The Art of Extract Making

The Art of Extract Making

A Kitchen Guide to Making Vanilla and Other Extracts at Home

40 Recipes and an Extract-Making Journal

Paul and Jill Fulton

Creators of VanillaPura

A SURREY BOOK

AGATE

CHICAGO

First printed in September 2023

Printed in China

Library of Congress Cataloging-in-Publication Data

Names: Fulton, Paul, author. | Fulton, Jill, author.
Title: The art of extract making : a kitchen guide to making vanilla and other extracts at home / Paul and Jill Fulton.
Description: [Chicago] : Surrey Books, 2023. | Includes index. | Summary: "A first-of-its-kind cookbook, featuring 40 unique and approachable extract recipes for both brand-new and experienced DIY extract makers"-- Provided by publisher.
Identifiers: LCCN 2023007766 (print) | LCCN 2023007767 (ebook) | ISBN 9781572843301 (hardcover) | ISBN 9781572848788 (ebook)
Subjects: LCSH: Cooking (Vanilla) | Vanilla. | Plant extracts. | LCGFT: Cookbooks.
Classification: LCC TX819.V35 F85 2023 (print) | LCC TX819.V35 (ebook) | DDC 641.6/382--dc23/eng/20230301
LC record available at https://lccn.loc.gov/2023007766
LC ebook record available at https://lccn.loc.gov/2023007767

10 9 8 7 6 5 4 3 2 24 25 26 27

Photos on pages v, 3, 5, 56, 65, 69 by Shutterstock
Photo on page 8 by Wikipedia
Studio photography by Nick Sokoloff

Surrey Books is an imprint of Agate Publishing. Agate books are available in bulk at discount prices. For more information, visit agatepublishing.com.

To Tommy and Sam,

When parents embark on a new journey, their children have little choice but to travel along. For the many moments that we have spent working on our business and developing this book, we thank you for your kindness, your sweetness, and your encouragement as our business grew.

You were only fourteen and nine when our first vanilla-extract-making party took place. You were both in the kitchen with us when the concept of our business, VanillaPura, was developed. You have been with us every step of the way, taking on jobs like adding labels to envelopes, packaging jars, organizing inventory, moderating our live online shows, and much more.

You are the very best of our family and we will be forever grateful for your ideas and your support along our extract-making trail.

We love you,
Mom & Dad

Contents

Pure Vanilla
& make
Something
SWEET!

Introduction

HOW IT BEGAN

In September of 2016, Jill and two of her long-time friends planned a holiday gift-making party. They selected homemade vanilla extract as the gift of choice. To make the extract, they purchased cute glass jars, vanilla beans, and vodka.

Buying the vodka was an experience unto itself. We live in Utah where liquor can only be sold in state-operated liquor stores, so we aren't accustomed to seeing vodka on Costco shelves or in grocery stores. A trip to the liquor store in Utah by three friends that aren't entirely familiar with vodka and its origins or its top-shelf versus bottom-shelf, three-times-distilled versus six-times-distilled characteristics was memorable.

Jill and her friends returned to our home, unpacked the vanilla beans, the vodka, and the jars, and began to make their holiday gifts. Paul was in our home office that evening with the door closed as the rising sound of laughter and the smell of vanilla began to fill the house.

The fun noises and energy emanating from the kitchen were different that evening from other evenings. (No, the ladies weren't drinking the vodka.) There was something special in the moment. An intangible warmth, sweetness, and kind enthusiasm radiated from our kitchen behind the smell of vanilla. There was so much noise and energy that our two sons (ages nine and fourteen) emerged from their rooms and came into the kitchen to be part of the experience, and Paul did as well. We learned that evening that it is impossible to smell the sweet, natural scent of vanilla without smiling.

Making extract in our own kitchen was a medium by which a special moment was born. Something of the simplicity of the task and the care taken in making these gifts brought our kitchen to life. And in a nontraditional way, vanilla beans, vodka, and cute glass bottles created a modern-day Norman Rockwell kitchen-centered moment with family and friends laughing together and enjoying one another.

In the seven years since making our first extracts at home, we have learned invaluable lessons ourselves and even more lessons from our 200,000+ social media followers that make extracts with us. Great vanilla extract can take over a year to make. Vanilla beans, like coffee beans, have entirely different tastes based on their origin and their quality. The type of alcohol you select has a major impact on the finished extract, and not just any alcohol will do. And nothing is worse than waiting an entire year only to find that your extract isn't made correctly.

This book is designed to help you avoid the same mistakes we made as we learned. It's filled with extract recipes, tips, and tricks to make sure your extract turns out exactly as you wish. It includes important details about vanilla beans and various spirits to help you make smarter extract decisions. But most importantly, we hope this book facilitates moments and memories with your family, friends, and loved ones. We hope you return to the kitchen to make something new and memorable and magical together.

Paul and Jill visiting a vanilla bean farm in Mexico.

Why We Wrote an Extract-Making Book

At the time of writing this book, there is not a comprehensive extract-making book that is available to help a first-time extract maker avoid costly mistakes. And perhaps for that reason, we see countless errors being made on a regular basis that are both expensive and avoidable.

Extract making is currently of great interest to many people, but there is no single source of reliable information. In fact, there is a sea of misinformation online about extract making. In our early extracting efforts, we followed much of that misinformation and we failed. We want to establish a quality extract baseline to make sure that your first extract is a lovely, sweet, and delicious extract. There is no reason that you should fail with your first attempt if you follow the instructions in this book.

In the past seven years, the two most recurring comments that we hear are:

1. Why all the fuss? It's super easy to make vanilla extract. Just put beans in booze and wait.
2. I have been waiting for a year, and my extracts still aren't ready. Why?

The recurrence of comment #2 would certainly be mitigated (if not eliminated) if more time was spent on comment #1. Yes, it is relatively simple to make great vanilla extract at home. But doing it right the first time does require some effort.

Let's explore the comment, "Just put beans in booze and wait." It begs the following questions:

1. What kind of vanilla beans? Grade A or grade B?
2. What vanilla bean origin? Madagascar? Indonesian? Mexican? Tongan? Ugandan? Ecuadorian? Tahitian? Indian? They all taste different.
3. What kind of alcohol? Vodka? Bourbon? Rum? Tequila? Brandy?
4. Does the different taste of each bean blend well with every kind of alcohol?
5. How many vanilla beans do I need?
6. How much alcohol do I need, and what proof should the alcohol be?
7. What kind of jar do I use? A glass jar or a plastic jar? Is a cork top OK? A plastic top?
8. How long do I wait?
9. How do I store the extract while it's extracting?
10. How do I know when my extract is finished?

In his book *A River Runs Through It*, Norman Maclean said that all good things "come by art and art does not come easy." Within this book, we intend to teach the art of at-home extract making and we will exert time and care in answering the ten questions above.

At-home extract makers don't have commercial equipment and facilities to delve into the science and chemistry of extraction to ensure that every extract is the same. Without expensive equipment, we must focus on the *craft* of making extracts at home, utilizing the tools available to you in your kitchen.

To make something new and beautiful is fulfilling. To give homemade extract to someone as a gift is to share the very best of who you are and what you believe you are capable of. Let others "put beans in booze and wait." We intend to help you make something much more sophisticated, something incredibly sweet, and something you can be proud of.

The goal of any type of extract is to maximize flavor and sweetness while minimizing moisture content for cooking. A lemon extract, for example, is much more concentrated than pure lemon juice. One teaspoon of pure lemon extract can provide as much sweetness as ½ cup of lemon juice, without adding ½ cup of moisture to whatever it is you are baking. The same is true with vanilla extract and all other types of extract.

To help you make the very best vanilla extract at home, the following chapters will explore the different species and origins of vanilla beans from all around the world. We will explore the histories, tastes, and applications of vodka, bourbon, rum, and other fine spirits used in extract making. We will discuss proper storage vessels and environments to ensure satisfactory extraction of vanilla beans. And finally, we will share dozens of extract recipes from basic, simple starting points to more intricate and complex extract recipes that include fruits, spices, cacao, coffee, and more.

This book is not intended to be a deep dive into the biology and cellular structure of vanilla beans, the chemical makeup of extracts, or scientific proposals of cellular-level vanilla bean harvesting and extraction methods. For a thorough scientific review of vanilla, we recommend *Vanilla*, by Eric Odoux and Michel Grisoni. We also recommend *Handbook of Vanilla Science and Technology*, by Daphna Havkin-Frenkel and Faith C. Belanger, as a thoughtful, well-researched, valuable resource. Within this book, we will provide a simple and broad summary of concepts to serve as a kitchen guide (not a laboratory guide) to extract making. We will help you understand vanilla generally, to aid with decision making as you create your extracts at home.

As you begin to grasp the general science of extract making, we hope this book serves only as a starting point. We hope that you take our recipes, concepts, ideas, and instructions and make them all your own. As you succeed, we hope you share what you learn with us, so we can all learn more together. We hope you smile, laugh, and enjoy the sweet journey that you are about to begin!

Vanilla Bean History

A vanilla bean, in all its glorious and sweet applications, is simply a bean. But not just any bean. It's a story of elegance hidden within simplicity. It reminds us to never judge something by its name or appearance alone but, rather, for what it truly is. A vanilla bean reminds us that we all have something within us that is beautiful and sweet and valuable to others. Extracting the sweet essence of a vanilla bean is magical. Yes, it is a bean. But this bean has a story.

At the time of writing this book, the vanilla bean is the second-most expensive spice in the world, just behind saffron. Why is that the case? Coffee beans and cacao beans are grown in the same region of the world. So why is the vanilla bean so expensive? What makes it different?

Vanilla is the second-most expensive spice in the world.

To answer that question, we need to take a quick trip back in time to understand the origin of vanilla.

The Totonacs of Veracruz, Mexico, are the first people in the world known to have cultivated vanilla beans. By the 1400s, the Aztecs had begun using vanilla beans to enhance the taste of chocolate.

When Spanish explorer Hernán Cortés discovered the spice in 1519, he brought a large supply back with him to Spain and introduced it to King Charles V and his royal court. Vanilla beans became instantly popular and vanilla bean farms quickly spread across Europe and into Africa and Asia.

Like many orchids, the *V. planifolia* (the vanilla bean orchid) is an epiphyte that lives on a host tree. It's a vine that grows rapidly up and around an existing tree but does not draw on the tree's nutrients. The vanilla vine can be up to three years old before it begins to grow orchids and then vanilla bean pods. The pods themselves require an additional six to ten months of growth before they can be harvested.

Edmond Albius

As Cortés's vanilla discovery spread across new regions of the world, early European, African, and Asian vanilla bean farmers planted their vanilla vines. But a problem soon emerged: the vanilla vines grew, and the orchids bloomed, but no fruit (vanilla beans) grew from the orchids. Why?

Cortés brought the vanilla vines and beans back, but he was unaware of one crucial necessity: the bees. But not just any bee would do. It had to be the Melipona bee.

Vanilla orchids are hermaphroditic, meaning they contain both male and female reproductive organs. Because of a plant tissue in each flower called the rostellum, which covers the stem, the flower cannot self-pollinate. In addition, the pollen on a vanilla orchid is highly inaccessible to most pollinating insects, so a typical honeybee cannot climb deep into the orchid. The social and stingless Melipona bee is small enough to move pollen within a vanilla orchid for fertilization. Without a natural pollinator, how could farmers ensure a vanilla bean harvest every year?

In 1841 a twelve-year-old boy named Edmond Albius, who was enslaved on the island Réunion near Madagascar, changed the world with a discovery that is still used today. With the help of a toothpick-sized stick, Edmond learned that a vanilla bean orchid could be hand-pollinated to produce a vanilla bean. A natural pollinator like a bee would no longer be needed to pollinate vanilla beans.

If your life's contribution is measured by the happy moments you create for others, then we could safely say that few other people on our planet have helped more people smile than Edmond Albius. His discovery paved the way for vanilla bean sweetness to cover the earth.

Today, in the absence of natural pollinators, laborers in vanilla bean farms around the world walk daily through their vanilla fields and look for orchids that have recently bloomed. Upon finding a bloomed orchid, they manually pull back the rostellum, insert the toothpick to access the pollen, and move the pollen to the stem previously covered by the rostellum to ensure fertilization. Vanilla orchids only bloom for a few hours in the morning, and if pollination does not occur by midday on the first day of bloom, the opportunity for that orchid to develop into a vanilla bean is diminished.

All that work, for one single bean.

A vanilla bean is the only fruit on our planet that is derived from an orchid. And nearly all vanilla beans today are in existence because a human hand-pollinated the vanilla orchid at the exact time that it bloomed.

Vanilla beans are grown all around the world in the bean region, or "bean belt," as coffee growers call it. This is the area of our planet that is 25 degrees north and south of the equator. The climate within the bean belt is the most ideal for growing coffee beans, cacao beans, and vanilla beans.

Nearly all vanilla beans today are in existence because a human hand-pollinated the vanilla orchid.

Vanilla Bean Species and Origins

VANILLA BEAN SPECIES

So, what's the difference between vanilla beans? Let's begin with a species distinction. Broadly, the three most popular types of vanilla beans in the world right now are *V. planifolia*, *V. tahitensis*, and *V. pompona*. There are more than one hundred species of vanilla orchid, most of which do not produce vanilla beans. In addition, there are various species of vanilla beans used in at-home extract making that we do not address in detail, such as *V. bahiana*.

The "V." preceding the species name stands for "Vanilla" which is to say, for example, that *V. planifolia* is the *planifolia* species of a vanilla orchid.

V. planifolia is the most common vanilla bean grown around the world, originating from southern Mexico and Belize. It is often called "The Vanilla." This is the Mexican vanilla bean discovered by Cortés and taken back to Europe and eventually to Madagascar, mainland Africa, Asia, and the rest of the world.

The *V. tahitensis* bean is growing in popularity due to its uniform smaller size, its durability, and its sweet taste with subtle, fruity notes. Originating in South America, it is a smaller hybrid of the *pompona* and *planifolia* vanilla beans. Many believe that because of its name it is grown exclusively in Tahiti, but that is not the case. Most *tahitensis* vanilla beans are grown in Indonesia, Ecuador, Papua New Guinea, and other regions around the world, in addition to Tahiti.

Finally, the *V. pompona* is a South American bean that can grow to a gigantic size by vanilla bean standards. One bean can grow to 12 or more inches in length and weigh more than 1 ounce. It has a ripe taste and aroma, reminiscent of an aged fig and dried fruits and flora. This vanilla bean species only recently started being used in at-home extract making. While it's a wonderful vanilla bean that results in a tasty extract in our experience, the FDA formally only recognizes *V. planifolia* and *V. tahitensis* in their definition of "pure" vanilla extract. So the *V. pompona* may not be used in commercial extracts just yet, but many at-home extract makers love the sweet taste derived from this unique vanilla bean.

While the species of each distinct vanilla bean will contribute somewhat to its unique flavor and aroma, the soil and climate where the bean is grown will determine quality and taste more than species alone.

VANILLA BEAN ORIGINS

Let's explore several vanilla beans based on their species and the region of the world where they are grown. There are many vanilla beans other than those listed here, but these represent a popular sampling of beans and their distinctions. They are listed alphabetically.

It's important to note that each vanilla bean has over three hundred flavor compounds, so people may experience these flavors and aromas differently based on their own palate or sensitivity to smells. One person may immediately notice the fruity undertones of a vanilla bean, while another person picks up the earthy, mocha, or cacao base. We approach the nosing and tasting of vanilla beans and extracts as one might approach the nosing and tasting of fine wines or spirits. Slowly, carefully, and thoughtfully we tried to tease out the various flavor and aroma notes. The descriptions below are how we experienced each vanilla bean. Your experience might be different.

Ecuadorian (*V. tahitensis*)

This is an exquisite vanilla bean with a unique flavor profile: a bold vanilla with hints of plums, apricots, and cherries. It has a durable outer skin protecting a rich center of sweet vanilla caviar. (Caviar is what we call the seeds inside the vanilla bean pod, as their look, shape, and texture is just like caviar.) Upon use, you will notice a floral vanilla smell and taste, while the subtleties of the fruits will present themselves fully after extraction.

Hawaiian (*V. planifolia*)

Most Hawaiian vanilla beans are grown along the northern shores of Hawaii and offer one of the most unique vanilla experiences. As with all vanilla beans, the predominant flavor is a sweet and soft vanilla. But the smells and tastes of tropical fruit bring this vanilla to life. A hint of mango, guava, papaya, and even a subtle undertone of cacao might be observed.

Indonesian (*V. planifolia*)

This is a popular vanilla bean for dark chocolate lovers. Indonesian *V. planifolia* beans have an earthy, strong, and smoky vanilla profile, contributing to chocolate and mocha notes that are perfect for dark chocolates, frostings, and brownies. These vanilla beans may also smell of dried fruit or raisins and they contain bold, earthy, woody, and dark vanilla notes with hints of dark cacao.

Indonesian (*V. tahitensis*)

V. tahitensis vanilla beans from Indonesia are known for their subtle floral aromas with fruity undertones. This is a great example of the impact of species on taste, since Indonesia grows both *V. planifolia* and *V. tahitensis*. The *V. tahitensis* beans grown in Indonesia have a light, crisp, and uniquely sweet vanilla taste that is great for fruit-based desserts, creams, and pastries. Surprisingly to us, they vary somewhat from the *V. tahitensis* that are grown in Ecuador, which seem to have stronger notes of plums or apricots—a great example of how bean environment impacts the taste of the same species.

Vanilla species, from left to right: *V. Peruvian pompona, V. planifolia, V. tahitensis, V. Mexican pompona, V. Mexican bahiana.*

Madagascar (*V. planifolia*)

This is often called Bourbon vanilla, and many believe its name is related to the spirit bourbon. However, Bourbon is actually the name of the region of islands that includes Madagascar, Comoros, and Réunion where vanilla beans are grown.

This vanilla bean has a classic buttery and rich vanilla taste. It has universal vanilla appeal and a wide range of applications in baking, brewing, and so much more. This became the world's most popular vanilla bean because Madagascar has historically produced more vanilla beans than any other country. Madagascar *V. planifolia* vanilla beans possess the traditional vanilla tastes and smells that most people are familiar with because they are the vanilla beans that most of the world has used for decades in vanilla ice creams, candies, sweets, pastries, and more.

Mexican (*V. planifolia*)

The climate and soil of Mexico contribute to a rich vanilla aroma and traditional taste, but with a slight spicy kick that hints of smoky caramel and chocolate notes. Sometimes a woody and a soft coffee scent are also present. This is usually a more expensive vanilla bean as supplies are limited due to low production within Mexico.

Mexican (*V. pompona*)

This is a large vanilla bean grown in the southern regions of Mexico. One bean by itself can sometimes weigh more than ½ ounce. It is full of vanilla caviar and is very sweet and aromatic. It tastes of dried fruits, raisins, and tropical, floral notes. Of course, it's primary taste and aroma is a dark, bold, powerful vanilla.

Papua New Guinea (PNG) (*V. planifolia*)

This vanilla bean is much like Madagascar vanilla beans. It boasts a classic, buttery vanilla taste and aroma. Given its origin in the lush, tropical jungles of PNG, you will notice soft floral undertones with a hint of tropical fruit, but just subtly.

Sri Lankan (*V. planifolia*)

Sri Lanka is home to teas and coffees made popular by its rich, floral soil. Vanilla beans from Sri Lanka are equally elegant. The bold vanilla taste of these beans is softened by a hint of dates. Behind the vanilla, you will pick up a cacao scent that is reminiscent of a chocolate-rich mocha. This bean also teases with hints of tea and other earthy, naturally sweet, and floral notes.

Tongan (*V. planifolia*)

Tongan bean cultivation is incredibly limited, making Tongan beans one of the most expensive beans on the market right now. Even at higher prices, they continue to be in high demand for their nontraditional vanilla flavor. They usually have strong cherry notes, an anise aftertaste, and a bold vanilla taste and aroma.

Ugandan (*V. planifolia*)

This bold vanilla bean presents itself with hints of raisins and figs along with mocha undertones. It's a brilliant combination of soft and fruity accents coupled with traditional vanilla aromas and tastes. It has a woody and dark vanilla aroma but softens into a fruity vanilla taste after it has been extracted. Naturally high in vanillin content, this bean boasts one of the strongest vanilla aromas.

This list of vanilla beans is not comprehensive. We name just a few to demonstrate the complex nature of each bean. There are many more vanilla bean origins that are not listed here, and each origin has its own defining characteristics drawn from the soil that nurtures its vines.

No two vanilla beans are the same. As you become more familiar with their differing tastes and aromas, you will find unique and original cooking applications for each type of bean and each type of vanilla extract. In the same way a coffee aficionado appreciates the differences in a Columbian coffee versus a Costa Rican coffee, you will grow to appreciate the differences between a Madagascar vanilla bean and a Tongan vanilla bean, and all the others.

When you begin making vanilla extract at home, don't just buy the first vanilla beans that you find. Do some research. Study the bean species and origin and make sure that the flavor profile is something that you are interested in.

No two vanilla beans are the same. As you become more familiar with their differing tastes and aromas, you will find unique and original applications.

Vanilla Bean Harvesting

There are seven stages of vanilla bean harvesting. Proper harvesting techniques lead to healthy, durable, aromatic vanilla beans. Given the delicate nature of their origins, the process of harvesting vanilla beans can't be rushed without significantly impacting the quality of the finished bean. Madagascar actually prohibits expedited cultivation of vanilla beans by enforcing nationwide laws that ban the sale of vanilla beans during certain months of the year. While vanilla beans can be made to look healthy, only time and temperature can ensure that each bean is dried and cured correctly to maximize sweetness.

TATTOOING

When the vanilla bean begins to mature on the vine and is nearly ready for harvest, many vanilla bean farmers will tattoo a small portion of their beans. Given the high price of vanilla beans, tattoos are used to mitigate theft and protect the hard work of the farmer. They are added with the use of a sharp thorn or needle by "poking" several small, superficial holes in the outer skin of the pod in the pattern of initials that identify the farm where the vanilla is grown. It is believed to be a good omen if you are fortunate enough to find a bean with a tattoo in your home.

A farmer adding a tattoo to a vanilla bean.

An example of a vanilla bean tattoo.

PICKING

Roughly six to ten months after the vanilla orchid has been hand-pollinated, the vanilla beans are ready to be harvested. At this phase they are green and odorless. They look like a large green bean pod that you may see in your own home garden. They are carefully, manually cut from the vine to ensure that the tip is not cracked and the pod is not opened in any way.

KILLING/BLANCHING

Once picked, the firm green vanilla beans are usually placed in boiling water. This blanching process ensures that the outer vegetative skin of the bean is killed, which keeps the bean from growing further. The vanilla bean pod will usually turn from green to brown within just one or two days of blanching.

SWEATING

Given the bean belt's proximity to the equator, it can be trusted to provide a hot sun year-round. The process of sweating the vanilla bean is done today the same way it was done by the Aztecs: sunshine and time. The vanilla pods are laid out individually under the hot sun during the day and then wrapped in blankets at night to "sweat" out

their inherent flavor and aroma. It is in this phase that the wonderful, familiar flavor and aroma of vanilla begins to present itself. Small vanilla beans cure quickly and can be damaged if left too long in direct sunlight. Larger vanilla beans require more time. As such, the sweating and drying processes must take place under regular, close supervision to minimize overdrying that can result in the cracking of vanilla bean pods. Most vanilla beans are typically sweated in direct sunlight for two to four weeks.

DRYING

Toward the end of the sweating process when the vanilla beans are sufficiently dark and dry, the beans are brought inside and air-dried in a dark room to allow the vanillin oils to sufficiently cover the vanilla bean. The process of air-drying in a dark room begins sooner for smaller beans that might be damaged by too much sunshine. It's the final step in creating a finished vanilla bean that is ready for commerce. Similar to sweating, this step of production can also last another two to four weeks depending on vanilla bean size.

The true art of fine vanilla bean cultivation happens in this phase. It is here, within shaded warehouses, that vanilla farmers gently and regularly massage every single vanilla pod between their fingers to free the oils and maximize the vanilla aroma and taste.

GRADING

Once dried, vanilla beans are laid out and graded based on their quality, shape, length, water activity, vanillin content, and moisture content and designated "grade A" or "grade B." Grade B is vanilla that is cracked or more dry, typically with a moisture content below 25 percent. Grade A is typically pliable and more oily than grade B, with a moisture content above 25 percent. The beans are then bundled by hand, separated by class, and prepared for shipment.

SHIPPING

When farmers ship vanilla beans to retailers in bulk, they will often send them wrapped in burlap or inside a container lined with wax paper. This allows the beans to breathe, and is also an expression of confidence in bean quality by the farmer. A properly cured, vanillin-rich, oily vanilla bean contains natural antimicrobial properties that keep the bean healthy and clean. This is how Cortés was able to bring vanilla beans back to Spain in the 1500s without the use of vacuum sealing and other food preservation techniques that we use today.

Most vanilla bean retailers wisely use modern technology to vacuum seal smaller quantities of beans for consumer use. By vacuum sealing, all the oxygen is removed. Bacteria requires oxygen to grow, so by eliminating oxygen around the bean, the likelihood of mold growth is very low. A well-packaged, vacuum-sealed bundle of vanilla beans can safely be stored in a cool, dry place for more than a year. A vacuum seal is also a way to ensure that the beans are safe and undamaged during transport to your home.

A finished vanilla bean arriving at your home is the representation of up to five years of cultivation and preparation. All of this makes the vanilla bean the second-most expensive spice in the world.

Selecting Your Vanilla Beans

CHOOSING A BEAN SPECIES AND ORIGIN

Now that you know the differences in bean quality, species, and origin, how do you select what bean to purchase for your first extract? There is no right or wrong answer to this question because we all have a different palate. However, there are certain guidelines that may be helpful to you.

Your first criteria should be based on your desired outcome. If you are looking to make a "safe" traditional vanilla extract, then you should begin with the vanilla bean that you are already accustomed to, which is likely a *V. planifolia* from Madagascar. The country of Madagascar produces more than 70 percent of the world's vanilla and is likely the primary source of vanilla that you are most familiar with. It's a rich and buttery vanilla taste and is always a great place to begin.

Your second criteria may be the desired application. If you are looking for a unique extract to add to pies, tarts, or fruit-based desserts, then you may want a more floral/fruity vanilla bean such as a Tahitian, Tongan, Hawaiian, or Ecuadorian vanilla bean. If you are thinking of dark chocolate or rich caramel applications, then a dark, earthy Indonesian bean or Ugandan bean may be your desired choice. If you are looking for something to accentuate ginger spice or pumpkin spice, then a Mexican vanilla bean with a hint of mocha and a spicy vanilla kick might be your bean of choice.

Blending two or three vanilla beans into one single extract is a way to capture the very best flavors of all your favorite vanilla beans at once. We will give a few examples of blended vanilla bean applications in our recipes.

The chart below plots the vanilla experience on a horizontal axis of buttery/creamy on the left to fruity on the right, and a vertical axis of dark/earthy on the bottom to light and sweet on the top. This may be a helpful way to choose where to begin. Remember that Madagascar vanilla is likely your baseline experience, so think of each vanilla bean on this chart based on its relationship to Madagascar's flavor profile.

VANILLAPURA VANILLA BEAN TASTE PROFILE GUIDE

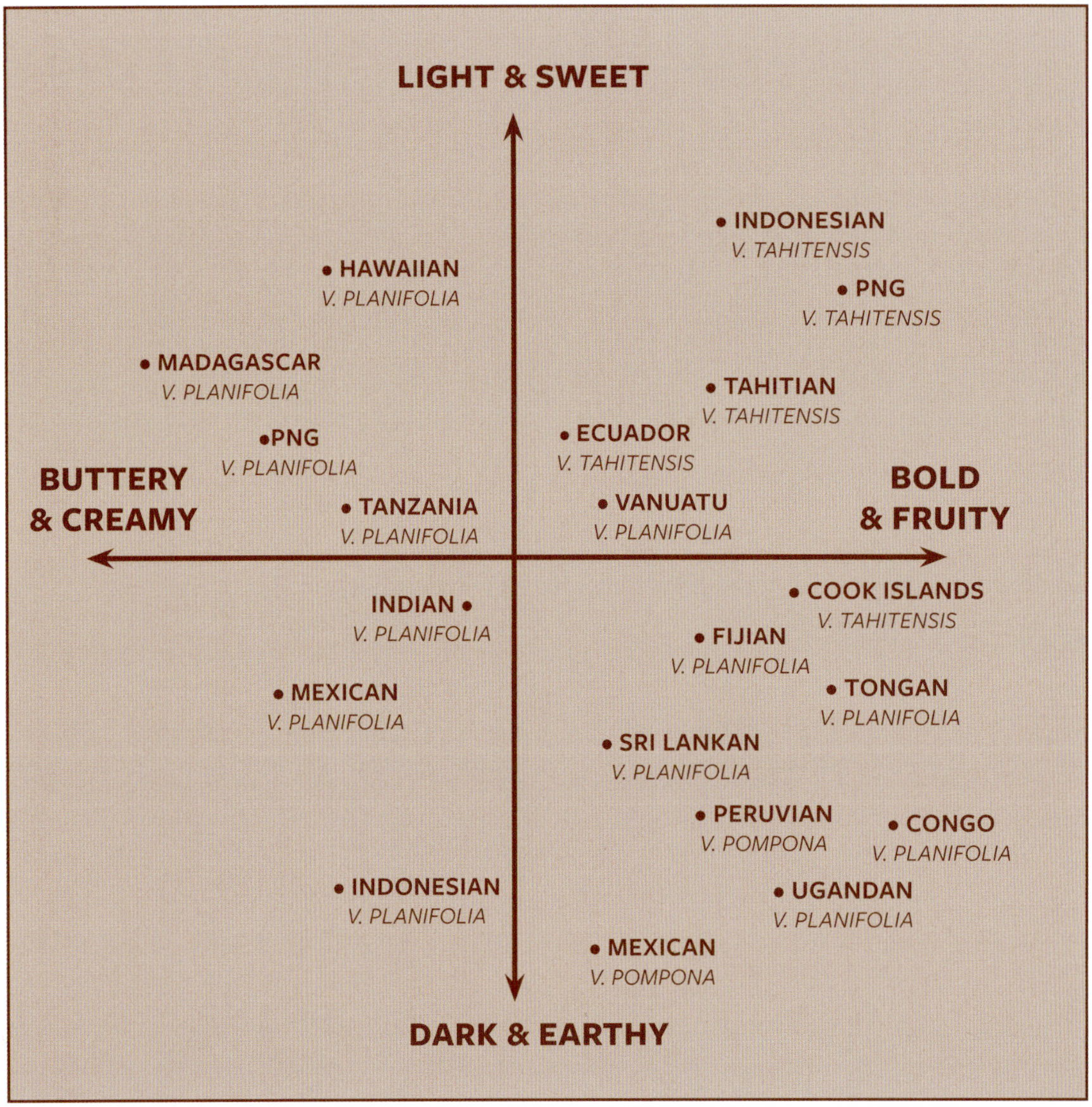

GRADE A VS. GRADE B VANILLA BEANS

Once you decide on the vanilla bean species and origin to use in your extracts, you must then decide whether to use grade A or grade B vanilla beans.

Grade A Vanilla Beans

Grade A beans (often called "gourmet vanilla beans") are visually more beautiful. They are plump, pliable, and full of fresh vanilla bean caviar. Their color is dark and chocolate-like, sometimes with hints of red. Their texture is soft due to their higher moisture content, which is typically greater than or equal to 25 percent.

Grade A vanilla beans are easy to slice open if you choose to remove the caviar for use in making vanilla bean paste, vanilla sugar, custards, ice cream, puddings, or any other creation where you want to see those beautiful vanilla speckles. They are rich with vanillin, the natural oil in the vanilla pod that creates the sweet vanilla smell and taste. Because of their high quality and versatility of use, grade A vanilla beans are typically more expensive.

Grade B Vanilla Beans

Grade B beans are visually less appealing because they are much drier and more brittle. They are susceptible to breaking and cracking. It can be more difficult to scrape the caviar from grade B vanilla beans, so they have limited applications, such as vanilla powder, vanilla sugar, or vanilla extract. Moisture content is typically equal to or less than 25 percent. The vanillin in a dry vanilla bean is more concentrated when rehydrated, but difficult to smell in its dry state. Because of their dry quality and limited use, grade B vanilla beans are typically less expensive.

Grade B and Grade A vanilla beans.

Which Grade of Vanilla Bean Is Best for Extract Making?

Both grade A and grade B vanilla beans can be used in making vanilla extract at home. Many vanilla extract aficionados will only use grade B vanilla beans for their extracts. The belief is that the drier grade B vanilla bean produces a much more concentrated extract taste. Commercial extract makers typically use grade B vanilla beans in their extracts, and the FDA guidlines reference the use of vanilla beans below 25 percent moisture content.

Other vanilla extract makers will only use grade A vanilla beans. In their experience, you can slice open the vanillin-rich grade A beans for an extract that is sweeter over time and provides more "caviar" to be used in the extract or other applications.

HOW MANY VANILLA BEANS ARE NEEDED TO MAKE EXTRACT AT HOME?

Based on FDA standards, "pure" vanilla extract needs to be made from 13.35 ounces of vanilla beans for every gallon of 35 percent alcohol. For those of us that don't want to make 1 full gallon of extract, how many vanilla beans should be used?

The simple rule of thumb calls for 1 ounce of vanilla beans for every 8 ounces (1 cup) of spirits.

There is a significant amount of misinformation online about the number of vanilla beans needed to make vanilla extract at home. Many instructions call for "5–6 vanilla beans in a cup of vodka," but this may not be the accurate amount. We have seen large vanilla beans where 2–3 beans are equal to 1 ounce. We have seen smaller beans where 15 beans are equal to 1 ounce. We have seen one *V. pompona* vanilla bean that weighed over 1 ounce by itself. Weight must be used as the unit of measure when adding your vanilla beans to alcohol—not bean count.

In addition, keep in mind that the weight of a grade B vanilla bean will be much less than the weight of a grade A vanilla bean due to the lower moisture content. This means 1 ounce of grade B vanilla beans may equate to 10–12 beans, while 1 ounce of grade A vanilla beans of the same width and length may only equate to 6–8 vanilla beans. This is another reason that grade B vanilla beans produce a very sweet extract: 1 ounce of grade B vanilla beans is simply more beans than 1 ounce of grade A vanilla beans. Advocates of grade A vanilla beans will explain how the quality and the cooking applications of a grade A vanilla bean are greater than those of grade B and, therefore, grade A should still be the bean of choice.

In our experience with DIY extracts, we have not found that grade A or grade B vanilla beans produce a more sweet or less sweet vanilla extract. We typically use grade A vanilla beans because they have more uses than grade B. If you are only making vanilla extract, then grade B is a more affordable option and will produce a beautiful extract. If you are using vanilla beans in your cooking, or using vanilla bean oils to sweeten your sugar, then grade A is a great bean of choice that will also produce a sweet vanilla extract.

Keep in mind that the added moisture content of a grade A vanilla bean can slightly dilute the alcohol content in your spirit. Selecting a spirit with a higher alcohol content of 40–50 percent may be advisable when making extracts with grade A vanilla beans instead of the 35 percent standard minimum alcohol content.

DOUBLE FOLD OR SINGLE FOLD?

The previously mentioned FDA guideline of 13.35 ounces of vanilla beans for every 1 gallon of alcohol is the definition of single-fold extract. It is the minimum amount of beans to alcohol required to yield what the FDA calls a "pure" vanilla extract. Double-fold extract is simply twice the minimum, or 26.70 ounces of vanilla beans for every 1 gallon of alcohol (or 2 ounces of vanilla beans for every 1 cup of spirits).

Does double fold mean that the extracts will be ready in half the time? Unfortunately, no. If you use twice the required amount of beans, and then you extract them for half the time, you are not giving the vanilla beans sufficient time in the alcohol to extract all of their beautiful flavor compounds. Complete, unaided extraction, in our experience, usually requires one full year. We suggest waiting an entire year for the double-fold benefit of complete extraction from all your beans. However, as an at-home extract creator, you get to choose. Since at-home extract making is more about the art than the science, if you like the taste of your double-fold extract after just a few months, then you can certainly begin using it.

How does double fold taste? Simply stated, it is twice as sweet. Twice the vanilla beans and twice the vanillin, in the same volume of spirit as single fold and extracted for the same amount of time. It's a vanilla lover's dream: an extremely sweet, concentrated vanilla taste.

A major benefit of double-fold extract is that it allows you to add twice the amount of sweetness to any recipe without increasing the moisture content of that recipe. In other words, if you want to double the amount of vanilla using single-fold extract, you must double the number of teaspoons (and moisture) used in the recipe. With double-fold vanilla extract, you can double the sweetness without doubling the teaspoons of liquid and, therefore, avoid altering your recipe.

We are often asked, "Is there really a difference? Since you only use 1 teaspoon of vanilla extract in most recipes, will you really notice if the extract used was single or double fold?" The answer is a resounding YES! And for those people that want to conduct an experiment at home, simply replace the 1 teaspoon of vanilla extract in your next batch of cookies with 1 teaspoon of water. How do your finished cookies taste? You will notice a significant, conspicuous lack of sweetness. A double-fold extract will demonstrate an equally significant increase in sweetness.

Most at-home extract makers begin with single-fold extracts. A single-fold extract provides a baseline for comparison with future extracts. It is difficult to fully appreciate the added sweetness of double-fold extract before understanding the expectation of sweetness within single fold. But beware, once you taste the richness of double-fold extract, you may never return to single fold again!

SHOPPING FOR VANILLA BEANS

You have completed your vanilla bean research. You have selected the vanilla bean species, origin, and grade that you want to begin with. Now where do you buy them?

Since extract making is done by bean weight, we never recommend purchasing vanilla beans by bean count. Depending on the size and moisture content of any vanilla bean, 1 ounce of vanilla beans can be 3 beans, or 1 ounce of vanilla beans can be 15 beans. Always buy your vanilla beans by weight to ensure that you are getting the most for your money.

For convenience, grocery stores or club stores are usually the first place that consumers look for vanilla beans. This is typically one of the more expensive and limited options. Grocery stores typically do not offer any variety of vanilla bean other than Madagascar and often sell beans by count rather than by weight. Grocery store supply chain management is expensive, and numerous middlemen create added costs. You will often find as few as one or two vanilla beans are sold at retail prices of ten to fifteen dollars. You can find them in the spice aisle in most stores under large brand names that you will be familiar with.

An online search of vanilla bean retailers will also yield numerous results, many of which offer an expanded variety of vanilla beans. Seek out those with positive customer reviews, a strong history, a fair return policy, product guarantees, and a large social media presence that will allow you to interact with other customers. Again, be sure to find retailers that sell vanilla by weight, and not by vanilla bean count.

Specialty vanilla retailers typically have less overhead and ship directly to you, so there are no middlemen. This means their pricing can be much lower. But don't sacrifice quality. Make sure they have a culture of food safety and utilize good manufacturing practices in commercial clean rooms for vanilla bean packaging. A confident retailer will typically have a no-questions-asked return policy and a 100 percent satisfaction guarantee, so you don't have to worry when you make your first purchase with them.

At the time of writing this book, vanilla beans can be found online for less than fifteen dollars an ounce for high-quality grade A and grade B vanilla beans. There are also very rare vanilla beans available for purchase from French Polynesia, the South Pacific, and other remote regions of the world that are more than sixty dollars an ounce. Indeed, never in the world's history has access to flavors and cultures from the most remote regions of our planet been available to so many consumers with just a few clicks of the mouse. Your extract and spice cabinet can easily include unique vanilla tastes from every region of the bean belt.

DISTILLER'S SELECT
WOODFORD RESERV
KENTUCKY STRAIGHT BOURBON WHISKEY
750mL
8496
2412

Choosing Your Spirits

ALCOHOL FOR EXTRACTION

In its definition of "pure" vanilla extract, the FDA has provided a minimum alcohol content requirement for vanilla extract of 35 percent. The remaining 65 percent of the solution is distilled and/or filtered water. (This is why water is typically the first ingredient listed on pure vanilla extract labels.) While no maximum alcohol content is established by the FDA, our own experience has demonstrated that anything greater than 50 percent alcohol (or 100 proof) does not speed up extraction and, in fact, can damage the beans and prohibit healthy and rich extract development. We recommend a 35–50 percent alcohol solution, which translates to 70–100 proof. Most vodkas, bourbons, rums, and other spirits fall within 35–50 percent alcohol content.

Vanilla extract is released through the essential oils within the vanilla bean. The process of extracting the essential oil into a solution is the essence of extract making. To extract is to create a solution by macerating and then percolating vanilla pods with the use of alcohol and water. The chemical reaction between the alcohol and the bean pod breaks down and "extracts," or transfers, the pure vanillin and other flavor compounds from the pod into the alcohol solution. Most of the vanilla flavor and scent comes from the vanillin that is inherent in the vanilla bean pod. The goal of at-home extraction is to gently transfer all of the vanilla bean's flavor compounds from the bean pod to the solution.

Sometimes, when adding grade A vanilla beans to a clear spirit like vodka, you can actually see the vanillin oil being extracted from the bean. It appears white and fatty and usually shows up in the first few days or weeks of extraction. The fatty vanillin continues to break down and finally dissipates completely into the extract spirit over time.

We use the term "spirit" instead of alcohol as we discuss extract making at home. By definition, a spirit is a distilled alcoholic beverage, usually with 35 percent or more alcohol and no added sugar. A liqueur contains 30 percent or more alcohol but also contains added sugars and flavorings. Beer is brewed and wine is fermented, rather than distilled. Both beer and wine can contain less than 20 percent alcohol. Using the term "alcohol" may infer that beer, liqueur, or even wine may work well for extract making, but they do not. Spirits refer to distilled alcohols (such as vodka, bourbon, rum, etc.) that usually contain sufficient alcohol content for extract making, and no added sugars or artificial flavors.

SPIRITS FOR EXTRACT MAKING

As you now understand, it has taken up to five years of delicate handling for a finished vanilla bean to arrive in your home. From vine growth to orchid blooming, hand-pollination, harvesting, sweating, drying, and classifying, great care has been taken at each step to ensure that your vanilla bean is healthy and ready to be submerged into a spirit for extraction. As such, your choice of spirit is a big, important decision that is a major factor contributing to the extract's final taste. How do you choose?

For those of you who enjoy an alcoholic beverage from time to time, you may already have a favorite spirit in mind. And to you, we always recommend choosing a spirit that you are familiar with and enjoy—one that has a predictable taste and that, in your own mind, will blend well with vanilla. Make sure that it contains 35–50 percent alcohol (70–100 proof). In most cases, we suggest avoiding spirits with artificial flavors. (We will speak about this later.)

For those of you who are not familiar with various spirits and how they may taste, we will approach spirit selection the same way that we approached vanilla bean selection. We will begin with three broad categories: vodkas, rums, and bourbons.

We should note that other spirits such as brandy, cognac, tequila, and various whiskeys from around the world can also produce unique extract flavors. We will focus on the three most popular categories within our review here.

Vodka

Vodka is a common distilled spirit for use in mixed drinks and cocktails. Why? Primarily because a good, distilled vodka is tasteless and odorless, allowing the other flavors within the drink to become the focus. This makes vodka the safest, most common spirit selection of first-time extract makers. Vodka will ensure that the vanilla bean's taste is the primary focus.

Most vodka comes from fermenting and distilling grain. This could be rye, wheat, corn, or various other grains. The quality of the vodka is directly linked to the quality of the grain and the number of times that the vodka has been distilled. While these are not the only two factors that make up a great vodka, they are important for extract makers looking for a clean spirit for their finished extract. The more the vodka has been distilled, the smoother and cleaner it will be. In vanilla extract, smooth and clean equate to stronger notes of vanilla.

What does distillation mean? It's the process of heating the beverage to remove the impurities and diluting components. Logic seems to imply that the more times the spirit is distilled, the purer it becomes, and that is true to an extent. However, distilling is a relatively simple differentiator. Spirit manufacturers are often anxious to distill six times or more just to be different from other four- and five-times distilled competitors. In our experience, once the vodka has been distilled four to five times, additional distillation is just for marketing and there is no significant taste or quality difference in your finished extract.

Rum

When we think of rum we think of pirates. But we should also think of sugar, a common Caribbean crop used for rum production and, hence, the association with pirates. And when we think of sugar, we think of enhanced sweetness. Anything distilled from sugarcane or sugarcane byproducts, such as molasses or cane juice, is a rum.

White rum is our personal favorite for first-time extract making. As with vodka, it is distilled up to five times and charcoal filtered. It is smooth and pure. At 35 percent alcohol, it will extract your vanilla pods effectively. Best of all, given its sugar-based origins, it will extract your vanilla beans with an enhanced level of sweetness. Given the typical uses of vanilla extract, a sugar-based distilled rum is the perfect spirit for at-home vanilla extract making. For desserts, ice creams, and toppings, a rum-based vanilla greatly enhances the sweetness.

Gold and dark rums are often used in extract making as well. These darker rums have heavy, smoky, and sweet tones that are great for caramel apples, toffee, and other deep and rich desserts.

Bourbon

We are often asked about whiskey and moonshine for extract making in addition to bourbon. Whiskey and moonshine can be used, but we focus first on bourbon for several reasons that we will outline here.

As the old saying goes, "All bourbon is whiskey, but not all whiskey is bourbon."

Whiskey is made all around the world. There are famous styles, such as American whiskey, Scotch whisky, Canadian whisky, and Irish whiskey. Whiskey can be great for vanilla extract, but we generally recommend bourbon to first-time extract makers looking for a smokier, darker vanilla extract.

Why? The answer is for consistency and predictability.

In America in the 1800s, the whiskey industry had a growing number of sophisticated distillers that were trying to make something consistent, predictable, and of high quality. However, they were competing with moonshiners and illicit whiskey distillers that were diluting their product to be price competitive. There was no gold standard in early American whiskey distillation.

In 1897, the American government recognized the value of defining what "American whiskey" would be to the world. They called it bourbon and they passed a law called the 1897 Bottled in Bond Act, which is still enforced today.

The law clarified proper bourbon production techniques. According to the act, bourbon "must be bottled and stored in bonded warehouses under the U.S. government supervision for no less than four years." The law outlined the following mandatory characteristics for bourbon to be called bourbon:

- Bourbon must be made in America.
- Bourbon must be 51 percent corn.
- Bourbon must be stored in new, charred-oak barrels.
- Bourbon must be distilled to no more than 160 proof and entered into the barrel at 125 proof.
- Bourbon must be bottled at no less than 80 proof (40 percent alcohol).
- Bourbon must not contain any added flavoring, coloring, or other additives.

In short, the act made the U.S. government the guarantor of bourbon authentication and provided a gold standard by which the world would judge American whiskey. Any bottle bearing the name "Bourbon" on the label must adhere to these standards.

We should note that whiskey and moonshine production and quality have improved significantly over the years as their traditions and processes have been refined. There are many great whiskeys on the market today that work well with vanilla extract. And we know of many modern-day moonshiners that make an amazingly sweet product that also works wonderfully for vanilla extract.

However, for first-time extract makers who want to try whiskey, we recommend starting with bourbon because the regulations under which it is made ensure a level of sweetness and consistency within your extract. Bourbon is clean like vodka but has a smoky/oak profile and is slightly sweeter, though certainly not as sweet as rum. It will bring out the sweetness of

SVEDK
VODK

the vanilla without overpowering the vanilla aroma. It enhances some of the darker/smokier vanilla beans like Indonesian and Mexican. Bourbon-based vanilla extracts are also wonderful additions to savory entrees like seared salmon, barbecue sauces, Italian pasta sauces, and much more.

So, Which Spirit Is Right for You?

The answer largely depends on the level of sweetness you are looking for. In concise terms:

- Vodka is flavorless, resulting in an unincumbered pure vanilla bean taste.
- Rum is sweet, resulting in maximum vanilla taste, aroma, and enhanced sweetness.
- Bourbon is smoky and slightly sweet, resulting in a rich and dark vanilla.

SPIRIT RECOMMENDATIONS

You may have already decided which spirit is right for you. A vodka may sound nice, or a bourbon may have intrigued your curiosity. Now it is time to select which vodka or which bourbon specifically. What brands are best and worst?

If you enjoy these spirits already, then you may have one or two specific brands in mind, and we would encourage you to use a spirit that you are familiar with. However, many extract makers within our online community do not drink alcohol. If you aren't familiar with the many brands of alcohol, then walking into a liquor store for the first time can be a bit intimidating. It was very intimidating for us when we made our first extracts. We had no idea where to begin the first time we walked into a large liquor store. If you feel similarly, then this section of our book is for you.

If you enjoy these spirits already, then you may have one or two specific brands in mind, and we would encourage you to use a spirit that you are familiar with.

We recommend that you begin with multiple types of extracts the first time, each in small quantities. Why? Because it takes up to a year to make extract, and after a full year, if you only made one type of extract, then you will only have one extract to try. If there is something that you don't like about it, you will need to wait another year to try another single version. We learned this lesson the hard way. If we could go back in time, we would have started with five or six (or maybe more) small bottles. You can then try a few different beans and a few different spirits, so in a year you will have multiple results to compare all at once.

We also encourage you to make your extracts with friends, each of you creating something different so you can compare your outcomes in a year. One of our favorite parties to throw at home is a vanilla extract taste-testing party. It's always a fun evening with friends and family and a great reason to get together and to bake something sweet.

As we evaluate our recommended spirit brands in the pages ahead, we will stick to our three primary spirit categories that we discussed previously, but with one addition. We will also discuss Everclear at the conclusion of this section, as it is an important ingredient when making extracts with fresh fruits.

> Remember: When selecting your spirit, "pure vanilla extract" must always be made with a minimum 35 percent alcohol, so you need to buy 70 proof spirits (or greater than 70 proof) to maximize vanilla bean extraction. We don't recommend exceeding 50 percent alcohol, or 100 proof, as higher alcohol content can damage your vanilla beans.

Rum

KIRK AND SWEENEY RUM

Vanilla Extract Grade: A+

This is obviously a top-shelf rum. It's pure, clean, rich, and sweet. It's stored in a sherry cask, and its production yields a taste that includes hints of caramelized sugar, sweet sherry, honey, and vanilla. For most extracts Kirk and Sweeney is cost prohibitive. However, a good vanilla extract will only be as good as the spirit used for extraction. We couldn't believe the rich, deep, bold flavors that came out of this extract after just six months of extraction, and even more after a year. The spirit only enhanced the natural taste of the beans, which makes this one of the best extract experiences we have ever had. Is it worth it? In some cases, such as vanilla flan, vanilla creams, or cream pies, a bold extract really enhances the taste. We set the bar very high with this delightful extract. It's clearly a top-shelf, A+ experience. Do you need a top-shelf expensive spirit to yield a great extract? Absolutely not, as the following reviews will demonstrate.

CAPTAIN MORGAN WHITE RUM

Vanilla Extract Grade: A-

We like white rum for two reasons: 1) it is sugar-based, which means you will get a sweeter extract, and 2) it's sweet, but the alcohol is mostly tasteless (similar to vodka), which means that after a year of extraction, you will primarily just taste the vanilla beans. This makes white rum a great kind of alcohol to use when experimenting with different beans. Try a white rum with a Tongan vanilla bean versus a white rum with a Madagascar vanilla bean and you will smell and taste the dramatic difference between those beans almost immediately. As such, white rum extract applications are almost universal. A Mexican vanilla extract made in a white rum can be used in almost any dessert, making this our favorite choice. Captain Morgan white rum specifically is a little less strong and more subtle, which results in a creamy and smooth extract at an affordable price.

BACARDÍ SUPERIOR WHITE RUM

Vanilla Extract Grade: B+

Given our affinity to white rums, we have tried multiple versions. While Bacardí is slightly less expensive than Captain Morgan, we don't believe that higher price always equates to better results. We did not see much of a difference in this case. The finished vanilla was fantastic but not clearly better than the Captain Morgan, so we felt that a B+ grade was appropriate. We also noticed that Bacardí had a stronger rum taste after one year of extraction—perhaps a slight kick or burn from its bold default taste—whereas Captain Morgan was a little softer. Some rum connoisseurs out there may appreciate the bold taste of a Bacardí over a Captain, but we liked Captain Morgan a little more.

CAPTAIN MORGAN SPICED RUM

Vanilla Extract Grade: A

Spiced rum will evoke memories of holiday eggnog or pumpkin-spiced cookies, and that is exactly what a spiced-rum vanilla extract can be used for. Banana bread, apple pie, bread pudding, gingerbread, etc. are all great applications for a spiced-rum extract. Everyone should have at least one bottle of spiced-rum vanilla extract in their cabinet just for the holiday season because it accentuates the taste of those familiar holiday flavors. If it weren't for the holiday-only niche, we would give this rum an A+. While we normally discourage spirits with artificial flavors, spiced rum is the exception. We will explore spiced rum even further in our recipes later in this book.

BACARDÍ GOLD RUM

Vanilla Extract Grade: B

Bacardí Gold has a unique rum taste. We could almost place this in the bourbon section below. It has bold, smoky, charcoal notes that are reminiscent of a scotch or whiskey, but it's sugar-based so it still errs on the side of sweetness. As such, an extract made with Bacardí Gold needs to be used for "darker" applications. We used Indonesian vanilla beans because they are inherently dark, smoky, and sweet. The result was a very rich and creamy extract that could be used in brownies, chocolate cakes, and chocolate frostings—perhaps even fudge or double-chocolate-chip cookies. This is certainly a unique extract, and its taste deserves an A, but its applications are limited, so we gave it a B.

CAPTAIN MORGAN DARK RUM

Vanilla Extract Grade: C+

Dark rum is rich, smoky, and powerful—so powerful that after six months of extraction, it was hard to notice the vanilla. After a year, the dark rum was still the predominant aroma. There were vanilla undertones, but they weren't bold or pronounced enough to overcome the rum itself. This could make the perfect vanilla extract to add a little kick to caramels, toffees, or dark creams, but that's a very specific niche. Still, it may be worth a try. Given its limited application and strong, smoky taste after one year, we felt that a C+ was appropriate. We also learned with dark rum (and later with bourbons) that some spirits require even more time beyond one year. In fact, if you're patient enough to wait for eighteen months or even two years, darker spirits can evolve into a rich vanilla experience that is sure to please. So while the extract grade for this spirit was a C+ after one year, it climbed to an A grade after eighteen months.

Bourbon

WOODFORD RESERVE STRAIGHT BOURBON WHISKEY

Vanilla Extract Grade: A+

As we did with the rum, we are going to start with a top-shelf bourbon. When developing a quality extract, you can't overlook a great spirit any more than you can overlook the importance of the vanilla bean itself. Woodford Reserve is one of the best bourbons in America, in our opinion. It has dark and smoky honey and caramel undertones, and since it's 51 percent corn-based, it's sweet. But there is something of the sweetness within Woodford Reserve that is special. Along with the caramel and honey, you can also taste hints of vanilla within the spirit itself. A Woodford Reserve bourbon extract made with an Indonesian or Mexican bean is the perfect rich, dark chocolate extract for darker desserts and even barbecue sauces and protein glazes to add a hint of sweetness. It's wonderful after one year, but after eighteen and even twenty-four months, this extract became one of our absolute favorites, with dozens of cooking applications. We have made Woodford Reserve extracts more than any others in our home.

BUFFALO TRACE BOURBON

Vanilla Extract Grade: A

A legendary spirit from a legendary distillery. This bourbon was recommended to us by one of our extract pros (an experienced extract-making member of our Facebook group), and it did not disappoint. Buffalo Trace bourbon blends well with Indonesian, Tanzanian, Mexican, Madagascar, and Hawaiian vanilla beans. It is incredibly rich with a delicate blend of honey and caramel, and can you think of two flavors more complementary in your homemade vanilla extract than honey and caramel? It has regular bourbon characteristics, just as a smoky undertone and a subtle bite, but it's a great bourbon base for first-time extract makers that are looking for something bold, but not overpowering.

MAKER'S MARK BOURBON

Vanilla Extract Grade: A

For its price, Maker's Mark is a great bourbon to begin with. It's made with a soft, red winter wheat instead of rye, which softens the bold tones found so often in most bourbons. What does that mean to you as an extract maker? It means that the vanilla has room to shine through and present itself within the complicated overtones of the bourbon. Simply stated, it's a solid mixture of smoky and sweet and allows for a pure, rich bourbon extract experience and a bold vanilla taste. We recommend this bourbon as a great starting point for new extract makers.

FOUR ROSES BOURBON

Vanilla Extract Grade: C

This is one of those instances where price and final quality did not match up. Four Roses is a nice bourbon and higher up on the shelf as it relates to price. But something about its bold spice and honey tone made it a difficult marriage with vanilla beans, in our experience. The final taste was too complicated and hard to find an application for. While it wasn't the worst bourbon extract that we ever tried, it certainly didn't meet its mark in our experiment. Perhaps with a more floral Ecuadorian or a PNG vanilla bean, you may have better results—or perhaps more time is needed than the eighteen months we gave it to mature.

UNNAMED BOTTOM-SHELF BOURBON

Vanilla Extract Grade: F

We went there. The bottom shelf. The cheapest bourbon that we could find. We won't name the brand here as we don't want to disparage its use. This bottom-shelf bourbon has a base of fans that enjoy it in mixed drinks, or they drink it neat around a campfire. For extract making, however, it was a total failure. In our experiment we used high-quality Indonesian *V. planifolia* vanilla beans and we waited a full year. We presented this extract to a team of chefs at a local culinary institute to see their reactions when comparing it to the Woodford Reserve extract mentioned above. Our goal was to determine how much the quality of the spirit impacted the final extract, and the result was immediately apparent. This was absolutely the worst extract that we've ever made. Our lesson here is to avoid the bottom shelf in the bourbon/whiskey category. You can often get away with using a low-priced, bottom-shelf vodka or even white rum, but with bourbon, the bottom shelf is a risky venture. Spend a few more dollars and buy a mid-shelf bourbon. You will be glad that you did.

Vodka

GREY GOOSE VODKA

Vanilla Extract Grade: A+

Grey Goose is a top-shelf vodka, and it proved to create a top-shelf vanilla extract. After a year, the vanilla bean taste became much more pronounced, making it one of the most fully rounded vanilla extracts that we have ever made. If you're going for a bold vanilla taste and an aged vanilla extract that you allow to rest for more than a year, this is the vodka you should use. It's made in France with a winter wheat blend that is truly unique. It's a smooth vodka that is distilled multiple times. We have learned over time that "smooth" and "distilled" translate to a more well-rounded vanilla extract, where all of the flavor compounds of the vanilla bean are able to present themselves unencumbered.

SVEDKA VODKA

Vanilla Extract Grade: A

If you don't want to spend Grey Goose dollars on your extract, Svedka is a great alternative. While this is not a top-shelf vodka, it will provide a wonderful final product that you will be proud of. Svedka is a winter wheat vodka like Grey Goose, but it originates from Sweden. It will provide a bold vanilla extract taste that becomes smooth and creamy with time. These extracts can be used with virtually any dessert or other food applications. The price is a little lower than Grey Goose, but the result is almost identical.

FLAVORED SMIRNOFF VODKAS

Vanilla Extract Grade: D+

We listed flavored Smirnoff vodkas as plural, as opposed to the singular. Why? Because Smirnoff offers many artificially flavored vodkas, all of which can be used for vanilla bean extraction, but with poor results. The grade of these vodkas is D+ not because of the brand's quality. (The taste of an *unflavored* Smirnoff vodka vanilla extract is an A, and we recommend plain Smirnoff vodka as an affordable vodka for extract making.) The grade here is a D+ because there are specific flavor applications available through Smirnoff that might tempt a first-time extract maker.

We tried making vanilla extracts with vodkas that have artificial flavors, and the outcomes

were very poor. At first glance, using a vanilla-flavored vodka to make vanilla extract sounds like a great idea to enhance the vanilla taste. Or perhaps a strawberry vodka for a strawberry-vanilla extract. It sounds lovely! However, in each of these cases our extracts tasted metallic and unnatural. Apart from spiced rum, we do not recommend using artificially flavored spirits for at-home extract making.

TITO'S VODKA

Vanilla Extract Grade: A

Tito's is made in Texas, is very affordable, and is surprisingly great for extracts. While not as smooth and velvety as Grey Goose, this vodka proved to be a great medium for vanilla extraction. We used Mexican vanilla beans with our Tito's vodka to see if we could still taste the mocha and caramel that are inherent in Mexican vanilla beans. An alcohol that is too strong will sometimes overpower the subtle notes of a vanilla bean. In this case, Tito's was gentle enough to allow the softer elements of the bean to shine through. This is a great vodka for the price.

Everclear – 195 Proof

Everclear is not a vodka, bourbon, or rum. It's in a category all to itself, made from a mixture of yeast, corn, sugar, and water. It is nearly 100 percent pure alcohol. There is a misconception in many online extract-making forums that Everclear will help your vanilla beans extract even faster, but that is not the case. In fact, in several home trials pure Everclear not only failed to extract the vanilla from the beans, but it ruined them.

Everclear does have its place in extract making. Several specialty extracts that we will review later call for fresh fruits. The water content within the fresh fruit will dilute the alcohol content of the spirit. To offset the dilution, the use of 195 proof Everclear is essential for these extracts to work.

Most fresh fruit contains moisture content of 85–90 percent, which is to say that in 8 ounces of fresh strawberries, 85 percent of their weight (6.8 ounces) is water. So, adding 8 ounces of fresh strawberries to 8 ounces of 195 proof Everclear effectively dilutes the Everclear by 42.5 percent, which provides an alcohol content level that is safe for extract making.

If using Everclear to extract vanilla beans or other items that are much lower in moisture content or completely dry, the Everclear must be diluted by 40–50 percent with pure water. This means that for every one part of Everclear used in the extract, an equal part of filtered or distilled water should be used. For example, if 195 proof Everclear is being used for vanilla extract, 4 ounces of water should be combined with 4 ounces of Everclear to provide the 8 ounces of alcohol solution required to extract 1 ounce of vanilla beans.

In short, the use of Everclear opens the door to a new world of fresh fruit extract making, but it can also be hazardous to dry fruit and vanilla beans. It must be used cautiously and somewhat scientifically in calculating appropriate dilution rates.

Of course, there are many other spirits that are not listed here. There are an endless number of brands that might all work for your extract. In addition, many of our extract-making pros have successfully used brandy, cognac, and even tequila, none of which have been discussed. Find a spirit and a brand that interests you and give it a try!

Deciding on Your Jars and Bottles

Selecting the perfect jar for your homemade extracts is no simple task. Of course, it needs to serve its purpose and function as a proper vessel to hold your extracts for more than a year. But can't it also be cute? What if the extract is intended to be a gift? Perhaps a bridal shower gift, a hostess gift, or a Mother's Day or other holiday gift. Shouldn't the jar reflect the care that went into its contents? Of course it should!

There are a few decisions that you need to make as you begin your search for the perfect extract bottle.

SHOULD I USE GLASS OR PLASTIC JARS?

Plastic is usually less expensive. And with the rising cost of vanilla beans, extract makers (even "pure" extract makers) are using plastic bottles more often. But plastic bottles have their drawbacks.

There are three primary issues with using plastic: permeability, leaching, and the environment.

Permeability

Plastic is more permeable than glass. That means O_2 and CO_2 are more likely to permeate a plastic container than a glass container. This is the reason that fine spirits are always bottled in glass, not in plastic. Plastic is reserved for spirits that will likely be consumed immediately, while glass is used for spirits that are intended to be stored and last for long periods of time.

Given the small serving size of vanilla extract used in your dishes, a large bottle of vanilla extract could last for many years once it is ready. As such, a glass container is recommended.

Leaching

Plastic contains at least two chemical substances: ethylene glycol and terephthalic acid. Both chemicals have a tendency to leach to a greater extent if used for storing any kind of alcohol for a long period.

With increased temperatures, those chemicals can leach into the fluid inside the container. Think of drinking a bottle of water after it has been in a hot car for a day or two. You're tasting those chemicals right now as you are thinking of it, aren't you? Not only can the chemicals be unhealthy, but they will also alter the taste of your vanilla extract.

Glass bottles, on the other hand, have high resistance to leaching given their solid surface. The dealkalization process that glass bottles go through ensures a smooth, impermeable, airtight environment that is important when storing liquids in glass, particularly alcohol-based liquids. For use in extracts, it's important to verify that the bottles are "food grade" or "food safe," which typically means that they contain no lead.

The Environment

Though progress is being made each year to produce higher-quality plastics, glass is still considered more environmentally friendly. The primary reason: glass can be recycled into new glass. It's reusable, repeatedly, and never loses its integrity. Plastic, however, can't be recycled into plastic. All plastic is new plastic and can only be "downcycled" into something like carpet pads and plastic lumber.

In summary, we believe that glass is the best option for both the environmental and product-quality reasons listed here. If you're an extract maker, we recommend using glass bottles. Of course, we follow this recommendation ourselves.

WHAT IS THE IDEAL BOTTLE SIZE?

As you consider the store-bought extract in your kitchen cabinet right now, it is likely quite small. If so, a small 2- to 8-ounce container may be all you need. But consider the amount of time that it takes to make extract: one year. In one year, how many store-bought containers will you use? One, two, or more?

You should plan to make enough extract to last twelve months. Once the first extract is ready for use, consider starting your next batch of extract to be ready in a year when your first extract is entirely consumed.

But beware, as many DIY extract makers find that their use of extract increases significantly as they make their own.

Finally, when considering the amount of extract that you want to make, you may want to purchase a jar that is larger than your desired volume. As you add multiple ingredients to your extracts, the spirit can be displaced. In some recipes that call for more than just vanilla beans, you may need a 12-ounce jar to make 8 ounces of extract. For 8 ounces of simple, single-fold vanilla extract, an 8-ounce bottle is usually just fine.

When considering the amount of extract that you want to make, you may want to purchase a jar that is larger than your desired volume.

CORKS OR NO CORKS?

If you are a wine connoisseur, you will know the answer to this question: why is a bottle of wine stored on its side? The answer: to preserve cork health by keeping the wine constantly in contact with the cork.

Cork is made from the bark of a tree called *Quercus suber*, or "cork oak." It's an all-natural material that can break down over time if it is exposed to moisture, then dried, then exposed to moisture again, then dried in a repeating cycle. By storing wine on its side, the cork remains moist and healthy for as long as the bottle is left unopened.

It isn't uncommon for fine spirits to also use a cork, but spirits are seldom stored on their side. In addition, spirits are not normally consumed quickly after the bottle is opened. A bottle of bourbon might be opened and used once, and then placed back on the shelf for months before being used again. So, why don't spirit corks deteriorate?

Spirits contain a higher alcohol content than wine. The air inside of a spirit bottle is always full of evaporated water and alcohol that is constantly and gently being circulated through the cork and keeping it healthy. There is not enough alcohol in wine to provide the same quantity of alcohol vapor at the top of the bottle to maintain cork health. The higher the alcohol content, the healthier the cork.

Another important consideration is that while corks are decorative and cute for use, they don't serve a functional purpose for extract making. They often collect the oils of the extracts and can be difficult to clean.

Are corks safe to use with extracts? In our experience, so long as the cork is new, we have never seen a cork deteriorate during extraction. We have successfully used many bottles with corks, and we like how the finished extract looks with a cork. However, once the bottle of extract is finished, we always throw out the cork and begin our next batch in the same bottle with a new cork.

METAL TOPS

Canning jars are used quite frequently in extract making. These are often the most affordable and functional jars that you can find. They are traditional and sized well for easy use. They are clear, so you can visually watch the extraction occurring over time. The open neck allows for easy insertion and removal of vanilla beans and other ingredients.

We have seen instances where the metal lids of canning jars rust during vanilla extract making. Typically, these are solid metal lids, and they are often on their second or third use. In addition, jar manufacturers often sell jars and lids for dry canning only and they do not include the air-tight seals that keep oxygen from entering the jar. Air and moisture can lead to rust. Be sure to read the box labels to confirm that the jars and lids can be used for wet canning. Fermentation jars are also great for extract making.

While we typically recommend a plastic lid instead of metal to ensure that rust doesn't develop, using a new metal lid or placing wax paper under the metal lid before twisting and tightening the lid on your extract jar are two steps that will greatly reduce the likelihood of rust. If you use wax paper under your lid, do not shake your extracts, as the ingredients will hit and tear the wax paper during shaking.

A CLEAR OR DARK BOTTLE?

Many extracts use dark, amber-colored bottles. This is done to mitigate the amount of light that passes through the bottle and interacts with the extract. In the case of grocery store extracts, which are exposed to light during transport and artificial light on store shelves, a dark amber bottle provides added protection.

For at-home extract making, we prefer the use of clear bottles for a few reasons. We like to watch the progress of our extract over the course of the year, and you can't do that with dark, amber bottles. We have also found that clear bottles are available in more options. When gifting our extracts, it seems that the cutest bottle options are usually a clear glass. Finally, our extracts are stored in places that are devoid of sunlight or any other light source, so the need for added protection from an amber bottle isn't necessary.

The Mother Jar

Seasoned vanilla extract makers have perfected the art of getting every ounce of sweetness (and value) out of their vanilla beans. Some of their tricks include adding sugar to the bag the beans shipped in to absorb the vanilla bean oil and turn it into vanilla sugar. They dry the vanilla beans after the first round of extract, blend them, and use them in vanilla powder. They harvest the caviar to make vanilla bean paste. And above all things, a great vanilla extract maker utilizes the Mother Jar.

OK, so what is a mother jar? In simple terms, it's a catch-all repository of all your vanilla "leftovers." It's usually a 1- to 5-liter glass jar with a sealed top that is near the kitchen but away from sunlight. What's inside of it? A lot of vanilla beans and spirits, and no two mother jars are the same.

What do you do with the vanilla beans in your finished bottle of extract when the extract liquid drops below the vanilla beans? You simply toss the beans from your everyday-use extract jar into the mother jar. When you make extract and have a leftover bean or two, you toss them in the mother jar. Then, as with regular at-home extract making, you simply add the type of spirit that you prefer. Maybe it's vodka, or rum, or a nice bourbon.

The result is a mother jar blend of extract that is totally original and entirely yours. Some of the very best extracts that we have made came from our mother jars—blends that included some Madagascar beans, some Tahitian beans, some Ugandan, Fijian, Tanzanian, Comoros, and Sri Lankan beans, and likely many others. Within your mother jar, you will discover extract blends that are entirely new to the world, invented by you in your own kitchen.

Does this mean vanilla beans can be used twice for a second extraction? While most of the value of the beans is used in the first extraction, there is still value in a used vanilla bean pod. We have seen vanilla extract mother jars that contain vanilla beans that are more than fifteen years old. We personally have mother jars with vanilla beans that are more than five years old, and the extract is delicious. We recommend that you always start a new extract with new vanilla beans for the very best results. But there is still sweetness within used vanilla beans that can be harvested by starting a mother jar.

Here are a few more mother jar tips:

1. Keep a log of what you toss into your mother jar, so when it turns out great you will know how to duplicate it.
2. While we don't recommend mixing spirits in high volume, it is certainly OK to toss vanilla beans in that were used in extracts with different spirits. You might have a Madagascar bean that was in rum and a Tahitian bean that was in vodka. It's OK to mix those. We just recommend using a single type of spirit to fill the mother jar.
3. Let your mother jar rest for at least twelve months, but once you start using it, you can toss in more beans as you have them or top off your spirit without disrupting the overall taste. You can simultaneously use and refill your mother jar, as long as you like the taste.
4. Consider how you will get your extract out of the mother jar when you're ready to use it. Since it's a big jar, you can't just pour it out on a teaspoon. You will need a small kitchen jar to fill for everyday use. You will likely need a stainless-steel kitchen funnel as well to pour from the large mother jar into the smaller everyday-use jar.
5. It's good practice to clean out your mother jar once or twice a year by pouring your extract through a strainer or a coffee filter and removing some of the oldest bean pods that may be deteriorating.
6. Buy a mother jar that is bigger than what you need. Just because you have a big jar, it doesn't mean you need to fill it entirely at first. The alcohol just needs to cover the beans. As you add more beans over time, add more alcohol. You will be surprised by how fast it grows.
7. Instead of one huge mother jar, you may want four to five medium sized mother jars to have four to five different experiments taking place. Perhaps one with bourbon, one with rum, and one with vodka. Or, one with only *V. planifolia* beans and another with only *V. tahitensis* beans.
8. Have fun! You may want to drop in a cinnamon stick for a month, or cocoa nibs and coffee beans for a month to add a mocha flavor. The mother jar is more art than science. It becomes a reflection of your own unique tastes. Make it yours and enjoy creating something new.

A Detailed Guide to Making Your First Vanilla Extract

It's time to bring everything together. With all the new knowledge and insights from the previous chapters fresh in your mind, let's begin the final exam. This is the sweetest final exam that you will ever take. It's time to make your first vanilla extract!

This section is a very detailed explanation of how a basic vanilla extract is made at home. All our recipes will reference various details within this section. When you have "how-to" questions about any specific recipe, you can return to this section of the book for detailed explanations.

There are eight steps to making your first, simple vanilla extract. They are:

1. Choose your vanilla beans. What origin? Grade A or grade B?
2. Select your extract bottles. How big? What kind of lid?
3. Decide whether you want to make single fold or double fold.
4. Slice your vanilla beans or leave them whole? It's up to you.
5. Choose your spirit. Vodka? Rum? Bourbon? Something else?
6. Fill your bottle with beans and spirits. Make sure the beans are fully submerged.
7. Store your extract in a cool, dark place away from sunlight for at least one year.
8. After a year, use your extract and reuse your vanilla beans in your mother jar, or use them to make vanilla paste, powder, sugar, or anything else that is of interest to you.

Let's elaborate on each of the eight steps to make sure that the process is clear and makes sense. Understanding the "why" of extract making will help to ensure that every extract you make turns out well.

STEP 1: CHOOSING YOUR VANILLA BEANS

Like coffee, chocolate, or any other bean-derived culinary treat, the quality of bean has the single greatest impact on the final product. Choose the highest-quality beans that you can.

The first choice you need to make is the vanilla bean country of origin. Vanilla beans grow all around our world within the world's "bean belt." Tahiti, Tonga, Madagascar, Comoros, Sri Lanka, Indonesia, Mexico, and other countries all contribute to our global supply. Each bean from each region has its own flavor profile reflective of the soil and climate where it was grown—from rich and fruity, to dark and smoky, to creamy and buttery. You can learn more about each region's distinct taste on page 12.

The next choice you need to make is whether you want a grade A vanilla bean or a grade B vanilla bean. Grade B vanilla beans are drier and less expensive. They are great for making homemade vanilla bean powder and vanilla extracts, but not much more. Grade A has a higher moisture content. These beans are fantastic for homemade extracts, pastes, and many other applications. They are typically a little more expensive. See page 29 for more detail.

STEP 2: SELECTING YOUR EXTRACT BOTTLE

First, determine the size of the bottle you need by estimating how much extract you will use in a year. Then, get creative and select the perfect bottle. Jars and bottles are a fun medium to express your personality and creativity. For some, it's all about function. For others, it's all about aesthetics. If you're making vanilla extract as a party gift or hostess gift, then the bottle needs to be small and cute. If you're making vanilla extract for your own baking needs, then it may just be about finding a bottle that is tried and true for your own use. The wonderful part about this step is that it is entirely up to you! Have fun. Be creative.

We recommend that you only use glass bottles that are "food grade." There are many reasons why you should use glass instead of plastic, such as environmental considerations and the impact on taste. We recommend using clear glass bottles so you can watch the extraction take place. When the extract becomes dark and amber, a clear glass bottle will give you a visual cue that your extract may be ready. See page 49 for more information on jars.

Remember to account for the space that the ingredients will take up within your bottle. If you want to make 8 ounces of finished vanilla extract, then you may want to select a bottle slightly larger than 8 ounces to account for the space in the bottle that will be occupied by the vanilla beans or other ingredients.

In addition, it may be advantageous with many extracts to make them in a simple canning jar with an open neck to allow for easy access to ingredients within the extract. Then, when it's time to use or gift the extracts, pour the finished extract into more decorative jars.

STEP 3: DECIDING ON SINGLE FOLD OR DOUBLE FOLD

How sweet do you want your extract to be? It's time to decide whether you wish to make a single-fold extract (roughly 1 ounce of vanilla beans for every 8 ounces of spirit) or a double-fold extract (roughly 2 ounces of vanilla beans for every 8 ounces of spirit).

We recommend that first-time extract makers begin with single fold so that you can develop a sweetness baseline to measure further extracts against. Starting with single fold will give you the added benefit of affordability and/or making multiple varieties of extract instead of putting "all your beans in one basket." See page 31 for more on single versus double fold.

STEP 4: SLICING YOUR VANILLA BEANS

This is the fun part, because in this step, your kitchen will begin to fill with the aroma of vanilla. It's a sweet, pure, subtle aroma that makes everyone smile.

There are multiple opinions about dicing and slicing vanilla beans. Some people choose not to slice to preserve the vanilla caviar within the bean for drying and powdering after the extract is made. While you will preserve more caviar by not opening the vanilla beans, it can also require extended time for the extract to be ready.

The goal with slicing is twofold: 1) to expose the inside of the vanilla pod for a faster, richer extraction, and 2) to ensure that your beans are cut to the right size to be fully submerged in spirits during extraction.

In some fruit, spice, or specialty extracts, vanilla is used as a binding ingredient that brings various flavors together into a smooth, finished single flavor. In these extracts, vanilla is not extracted fully but is extracted sufficiently to soften the flavor compounds of other competing ingredients. In these recipes, cutting the vanilla bean may be preferred to maximize vanilla flavor in a shorter amount of time.

To expose the inner pod of the vanilla bean, simply take a sharp knife and slice open the bean lengthwise from the top of the pod down to the bottom. You will see thousands of small seeds that we call "vanilla caviar."

Then, to ensure that your beans are fully submerged in the spirit within the bottle you have chosen, simply look at the extract container that you are going to use and make sure that you cut the beans to a size that is less than the level of spirits in your container. You want 100 percent of your vanilla beans to be fully submerged during extraction. (If you aren't dicing your beans, you can tie them in a knot or bend them to fit within your bottle.)

STEP 5: CHOOSING YOUR SPIRIT

Second only to the type of bean you are using, the type of spirit that you choose will have a dramatic impact on the final taste. Vodka is tasteless and odorless and will allow the natural vanilla scent to shine through. Rum is sugar-based and will add enhanced sweetness. Bourbon adds complexity to your extract, including notes of caramel, honey, and smoky oak.

Alcohol content should be no less than 35 percent (70 proof) and no more than 50 percent (100 proof) to ensure the sweetest, purest vanilla extract outcome. See page 35 for a detailed explanation of alcohol content.

Remember, if your extract incorporates fresh produce with high moisture content, you will need to use a spirit with a high alcohol content (such as Everclear) to account for the dilution that will occur with the moisture introduced from the fresh produce. For extracts with only vanilla beans and dry ingredients, a spirit with 35–50 percent will work just fine. See page 46 for more details about the use of Everclear in extract making.

STEP 6: FILLING YOUR EXTRACT BOTTLE

Once you have selected your bottle and your spirit and you have sliced (or tied or folded) your vanilla beans, it's time to fill the bottle. It might be helpful to use a funnel to ensure that the spirit doesn't spill outside of the bottle. Your beans may absorb some of the spirit in the first few weeks, so watch it closely and add more spirits if the level drops below the tops of the vanilla beans.

Make sure that your vanilla beans are completely submerged in the spirit to maximize extraction. If your bottle has a small neck, you can use kitchen tweezers or a single chopstick to push the vanilla beans down further into the bottle.

STEP 7: STORAGE AND TASTE TESTING

Extraction takes time and patience. Find a place in your home that is cool with limited to no sunlight. Set your extract on the shelf and slowly walk away from the bottle. It's hard to leave it alone after all that work, but it needs to be left alone for extraction to occur. Some people like to shake their vanilla bottles once a week, or more or less often. While shaking does seem to speed up extraction slightly, we typically leave ours alone and allow the alcohol and vanilla beans to do their thing. We recommend a monthly check-in to open and burp the bottles and to smell how they are advancing. It is always fun to peek in and watch the progress.

With the highest-quality vanilla beans and spirits, your extract could be ready in as little as six to nine months, but the longer you wait, the richer and creamier the extract becomes. We recommend waiting a full year, but we recognize that many extract makers begin using their extracts sooner.

Look at your extract regularly. Top off the spirit if you see that the fluid level is dropping. Sometimes the vanilla beans or other ingredients will absorb the alcohol, causing the alcohol level to drop. Topping off the spirit in the first month or two won't affect the outcome.

It is OK to open the bottle and smell the extracts regularly. One sign that your extract is nearing completion is the decrease in the smell of alcohol and the increase in the smell of vanilla.

You may notice that your extract is cloudy within the first few weeks or months of extraction. This may happen as the oils of the vanilla bean interact with the spirit. Over time, the cloudiness will dissipate. As extracting begins you may also notice the presence of off-white fatty matter emerging out of your vanilla beans. This is the vanillin oils being extracted from the pod, and they will dissipate over time.

If you think that your extract is ready, you can conduct a simple taste test by adding 1–2 drops of extract to a tablespoon of milk or milk alternative. Stir the milk and let it sit for one or two minutes, and then drink the milk. (This can also be done with whipped cream.) If the primary taste is sweet vanilla, then your extract is ready. If you still taste more alcohol than vanilla, then you need to give your extract a little more time, typically at least one more month.

STEP 8: USE AND REUSE

Now you've waited long enough and it's time to start using your homemade extract. There are a few things to remember as you begin.

You can begin using your extracts with the vanilla beans still in the bottle. This will add enhanced sweetness to your extract over time. However, as you use more extract, the vanilla beans will eventually become exposed. You can continue to cut the vanilla beans into smaller pieces so they remain submerged for as long as possible. Once the vanilla beans are exposed and can no longer be cut, it is best to remove them.

If you sliced your vanilla beans, the bottom of your bottle will contain a lot of vanilla bean caviar. Some people love vanilla caviar and others don't. If you fall into the latter category, then simply pour all your extract from the bottle into a measuring cup through a coffee filter or a cheesecloth. This will remove all the beans and the caviar, and it will make the extract clean and easy to pour. (The vanilla beans will feel very slimy. That's 100 percent normal after sitting in alcohol for months.)

Finally, take your used beans and dry them for vanilla powder, squeeze out the caviar for vanilla paste, ice cream, custards, or pudding, or place your used beans in a large jar and cover them with your spirit of choice to begin making your vanilla extract mother jar. See page 54.

Troubleshooting

We are contacted quite frequently by extract makers that started their extracts months or even years ago with bad advice. They are dissatisfied with the taste and aroma of their extract and worry that all that time and money has gone to waste. We tell them to not despair and to please not throw out all their work! There are steps that you can take to fix your troubled extracts, and these steps may not require a lot of time or money.

Problem: My extracts are one year old, but they still taste and smell "boozy."
Remember that the number one ingredient of each extract is alcohol, so the "boozy" taste and smell is always present. If you taste the extract directly from the bottle, it will taste a bit boozy. You need a medium like milk or whipped cream. Add a couple drops of your extract to 1 tablespoon of milk, stir, wait for one minute, and then take a sip. Vanilla should be the predominant flavor. If you still don't like the taste, you may just need a little more time. Let the extract sit for another month and taste test again.

Problem: I didn't weigh my beans and I'm not sure if I had the correct amount to begin with.
On average, 1 ounce of vanilla beans is usually 5–8 beans, but it can vary based on bean size. So, if you have fewer than 5–8 beans in every 8 ounces (1 cup) of spirits, then you likely have too few vanilla beans. The solution here is to simply add more beans and wait a little longer. You won't need to wait an entire year since your first vanilla beans have been extracting. After adding more beans, conduct a taste test every month until the extract tastes as you wish.

Problem: I weighed my vanilla beans and have waited a year, but I still don't love the taste.

Some extract makers are so accustomed to commercial extracts, which often include sugar or corn syrup, that the pure extract taste of just alcohol and vanilla beans is initially uncomfortable to them. A teaspoon of sugar stirred gently into 8 ounces of extract will typically suffice to soften the taste of the alcohol.

For those of you who don't wish to add sugar, small oak blocks or oak cubes can also be used. These oak products can be found online and dropped into your extracts for a few days or weeks to soften the taste. American, French, and Hungarian oak is used by fine spirit makers to store their whiskeys, rums, and other spirits. The oak naturally mellows out the alcohol taste and softens the bite. When using oak blocks, you will want to taste test your extracts daily, as the taste is altered quickly and dramatically by the oak, especially if the oak is previously charred.

Problem: It has been several months or even a year since starting my extract, and it hasn't even turned to a dark amber yet.

This problem is typically the one of greatest concern. Sometimes it's a simple case of someone getting bad advice and putting one or two vanilla beans into an entire bottle of vodka. When this is the case, the solution is to simply add more vanilla beans, per the recipes listed here, and wait.

If the correct amount of vanilla was used from the beginning and the solution hasn't changed to a dark amber after a few months, then the problem may be more significant. It may be that you used an alcohol solution that did not have enough alcohol (meaning it was less than 35 percent) or, worse, it had too much alcohol (well over 50 percent).

If the beans have been sitting in too little alcohol, they can be removed and added to new alcohol and the extraction should begin to happen immediately. If the beans have been in too much alcohol, then they may be ruined. We have seen this happen when extract makers use undiluted Everclear 195 proof or 150 proof. The high alcohol content seems to burn the vanilla beans. While the burnt beans can still be dried and converted into vanilla bean powder or possibly vanilla sugar, we don't recommend that they be used in another extract. In this case, you will need to begin again, unfortunately.

These are important examples that demonstrate why it is imperative to begin your first extract correctly. Too many people have contacted us over the years requesting help because they followed advice given online by someone who said, "What's so difficult? Just put beans in booze and wait."

Recipes

The simple art of extract making has completely changed our lives. At the time of writing this book, we have over 200,000 social media followers that constantly share tips, advice, and delicious new recipes that we would have never considered on our own. Most importantly, our extract-making journey has forged friendships and associations with wonderful people around the world. We have extract-making friends in more than twenty countries and in all fifty United States and all U.S. outlying regions who have introduced us to new extract recipes and applications.

Since extract making is a rapidly growing craft, we learn new lessons and experience new breakthroughs every single day because the general principles of extract making have endless applications. Alcohol is used to make almond extracts, herb extracts, fruit extracts, and so much more. So, while you will find many vanilla extract recipes in this book, there are several other types of extracts, and all have different applications.

"A recipe has no soul. You, as the cook, must bring soul to a recipe." —Thomas Keller

We incorporate the use of both fresh fruit and dried fruit in several specialty extracts. Dried fruits will typically provide the most concentrated taste in finished extracts. Because they have low or no moisture content, any spirit can be used for extraction. But dried fruits can also be very expensive. Fresh fruits are an affordable alternative when they are in season, but they require the use of a high-alcohol-content Everclear to offset their high moisture content.

Fruits typically extract faster, so the extract recipe requires that extracted fruits are removed and new fruit is added a second or even third time. Within our recipes, when you see a "(×2)" or "(×3)" next to an ingredient, particularly fresh or dried fruits, it means you will be adding that same ingredient in the same quantity again later, after a period of a few weeks or a few months.

If you choose to use fruit or specialty extracts in baked goods, you should use them in place of the vanilla extract in the recipe, not in addition to it. In other words, if your cake recipe calls for 1 teaspoon of vanilla extract and you wish to use your homemade strawberry extract instead, simply replace the 1 teaspoon of vanilla extract with strawberry extract. If you add 1 teaspoon of strawberry extract in addition to the 1 teaspoon of vanilla extract, then you have doubled the amount of moisture introduced by extracts in your recipe, which may affect the outcome of your cake.

In the case of creams, frostings, glazes, sauces, and other non-baked goods, you can add extracts more liberally since the added moisture will not impact the outcome as it might with baked goods.

We recognize that there are various types of DIY crafts that use techniques similar to extraction. For example, the term "tinctures" is used quite frequently in extract-making circles. Tinctures are like extracts, in that alcohol is used as the solution that "extracts" the flavor from the herb, bark, or spice. Alcohol content in a tincture can be as low as 20 percent and much higher than 50 percent.

The term "infusion" is used when candies (like Werther's Originals) are placed in alcohol for some period to create an extract-like product. With an infusion, the product dissolves within the alcohol rather than having its oils extracted.

An "emulsion" is another term that is used when two differing liquids are combined, like oil and vinegar, or a soft candy or sauce and an alcohol.

We refer to all our recipes as "extracts" in that they follow the FDA standard for vanilla extract in terms of the quantity of product being extracted and the minimum alcohol content of 35 percent that is always used. We recognize that some of our specialty extracts incorporate infusions and emulsions as well, as you will see later, but we still call them extracts for simplicity.

Our extract recipes in this book are divided into four groups: vanilla; chocolate, caramel, and coffee; fruit; and nut and spice.

To make many of the extracts, there are several kitchen tools that you will need to have nearby, some of which are essential, and others which are nonessential but helpful:

ESSENTIAL

- Cutting board
- Kitchen scale
- Sharp knife
- Funnel
- Scissors
- Fine-mesh strainer
- Measuring cups
- Measuring spoons
- Peeler

NONESSENTIAL

- Long tweezers
- Chopsticks
- Kitchen mallet
- Cheesecloth or coffee filters
- Sous vide cooker
- Nut and spice grinder
- Fermentation jar and weight
- Mortar and pestle

To help you stay organized, we have included a vanilla extract journal at the end of this book to help you track your extract experiments and progress over time. You will be amazed at how quickly every empty shelf in your home becomes a storage place for a new extract!

We hope you enjoy making and using each of these extracts as much as we do. You will notice that we have included some of our favorite quotes about sweetness throughout the recipes. They remind us of how sweet a finished extract is and how sweet the people are that we have made extracts with.

Vanilla Extracts

SVEDKA
VODKA

Your First Vanilla Extract

Makes about 8 ounces of extract | Extract time: 12 months | Jar size: 8 ounces or larger

If you haven't made pure, sweet, real vanilla extract before and you are wondering where or how to begin, this simple recipe is for you. This will create a traditional vanilla extract that will be entirely familiar to you. It utilizes Madagascar vanilla beans, which are the buttery and creamy classic vanilla beans that you likely already know and love. It also uses vodka, which is a flavor-free spirit that will allow the pure taste of the vanilla bean to really shine through. Its applications in cooking and baking are limitless.

1 ounce Madagascar *V. planifolia* vanilla beans

8 ounces vodka

1. Using a kitchen scale, weigh 1 ounce of vanilla beans. Slice the vanilla beans lengthwise to expose the caviar and cut the beans into pieces small enough to fit into the jar, or leave them whole if preferred. (See page 61 for more information about the decision to cut or not cut.) Place the beans in the jar.

2. Pour the vodka into the jar over the vanilla beans, ensuring that each bean is fully submerged. If the neck of the jar is small, then use a funnel to avoid spilling.

3. Close and seal the jar tightly with its lid. Store the jar in a cool, dark place in your home for up to 12 months.

After 12 Months

4. Taste test your extract to determine if it is ready by adding 1–2 drops of extract to 1 tablespoon of milk or milk alternative. If you like the taste, then your extract is now ready for use. If not, continue to store and taste test at 1-month intervals.

5. Remove the beans before use or leave them in the jar for added sweetness over time, making sure they always stay fully submerged in the spirit. If you choose, you can pour your finished extract into a more decorative jar for use.

"Patience is bitter, but its fruit is sweet."
—Jean-Jacques Rousseau

Note: Extract shelf life is at least 4 years when stored in a cool, dark place to prevent alcohol evaporation. We have seen extracts last more than 20 years when stored properly.

The Autumn Breeze Vanilla Extract

Makes about 8 ounces of extract | Extract time: 12 months | Jar size: 16 ounces or larger

Let's introduce a more complicated extract. This vanilla extract was developed to be a sweet, rich, and totally unique extract that can be used during the holidays for all your favorite treats. It incorporates some of our favorite holiday flavors and aromas that will evoke memories of hot cider, gingerbread, and more. Most importantly, it will enhance the flavor of all those traditional and sweet holiday classics. This recipe was inspired by one of our favorite extract-making friends, Starlette.

1 ounce Ecuadorian *V. tahitensis* vanilla beans, or any vanilla bean with fruity and floral notes

1 small ginger root

½ whole nutmeg

4 dried apple slices (×2)

4 dried orange slices (×2)

¼ cup dried cranberries (×2)

2 teaspoons allspice berries

1 teaspoon whole cloves

8 ounces Bacardí Gold rum

1. Place the whole vanilla beans in the jar. Do not cut or slice them. Bend them or tie them in a knot to ensure that they will be submerged in the alcohol.

2. Cut the ginger root in half, peel it, and slice it into small pieces. Add the ginger to the jar.

3. Place the nutmeg on a cutting board and cover with a dish towel. Using a kitchen mallet, break the nutmeg into small pieces, then add the nutmeg pieces to the jar.

4. Add the apples, oranges, cranberries, allspice berries, and cloves to the jar, then carefully pour the spirit over all the ingredients.

5. Seal the jar tightly and give it a gentle shake. Store the jar in a cool, dark place for 1 month.

After 1 Month

6. Remove the apples, oranges, and cranberries. If they are difficult to remove, you may pour the entire jar through a strainer to capture the used ingredients. Press the absorbed alcohol out of the fruits and back into the extract before discarding them.

7. Add new apples, oranges, and cranberries in the same quantity (4 slices each of dried apple and dried orange and ¼ cup of dried cranberries).

8. Reseal the jar, give it a gentle shake, and store for another month.

After 2 Months

9. Remove the apples, oranges, and cranberries, but do not replace them.

10. Reseal your jar with all other ingredients still inside, and store the jar in a cool, dark place for 10 months, shaking once or twice a month.

After 12 Months

11. Taste test your extract. Refer to taste testing on page 64.

12. Remove and discard the ginger, nutmeg, allspice, and cloves by pouring your extract through a coffee filter or a strainer, then return the extract to the jar. Either remove the beans or leave them in if preferred, ensuring that they are cut or folded small enough to remain submerged in the alcohol.

Winter Spice Extract

Makes about 8 ounces of extract | Extract time: 12 months | Jar size: 10 ounces or larger

This extract can be used in beverages like hot ciders and pumpkin-spiced drinks, savory wintertime dishes like hams and sweet potatoes, and our favorite wintertime baked goods like cakes, chocolates, breads, rolls, and more. We use two species of vanilla beans from the same region of the world, so you can experience the differences between the earthy *V. planifolia* and the fruity *V. tahitensis* vanilla beans.

½ ounce Indonesian *V. planifolia* vanilla beans

½ ounce Indonesian *V. tahitensis* vanilla beans

1 whole nutmeg

1 Ceylon cinnamon stick (Cassia cinnamon will also work)

1 teaspoon whole allspice berries

1 tablespoon whole star anise

8 ounces 70–100 proof vodka

1. Place the vanilla beans in the jar, cut or uncut depending on your preference.

2. Place the nutmeg on a cutting board and cover with a dish towel. Using a kitchen mallet, break the nutmeg into small pieces, then add the nutmeg pieces to the jar.

3. Break the cinnamon stick in half and add both halves to the jar. Add the allspice berries and star anise to the jar, then pour the vodka into the jar, making sure the beans are entirely submerged.

4. Seal the jar tightly and store it in a cool, dark place for 1 month.

After 1 Month

5. Remove both halves of the cinnamon stick.

6. Leave all other ingredients in the extract, reseal the jar, and store for 3 more months.

After 4 Months

7. Remove the nutmeg and allspice berries by pouring the extract through a strainer or coffee filter. Return the extract and the vanilla beans to the jar.

8. Reseal the jar and store for 8 more months.

After 12 Months

9. Taste test your extract. Refer to taste testing on page 64.

10. When ready to use, either remove the beans or leave them in if preferred, ensuring that they are cut or folded small enough to remain submerged in the alcohol.

Indonesian and Tahitian Vanilla Blend with Vodka

Makes about 8 ounces of extract | Extract time: 12 months | Jar size: 8 ounces or larger

Often with vanilla extract making, less is more, and simplicity is elegant and delicious. So it is with this extract that relies entirely on the unique differences between two vanilla beans: Indonesian and Tahitian.

Indonesian V. *planifolia* vanilla beans are known for their dark, smoky, earthy, and mocha-like vanilla richness and sweetness. Tahitian V. *tahitensis* vanilla beans, on the other hand, are known for their subtle notes of dried tropical fruits and flora. When you combine the two with a pure vodka, you have an extract that is unique and wonderful for use in dark chocolates, frostings, caramels, brownies, and more.

½ ounce Indonesian *V. planifolia* vanilla beans

½ ounce Tahitian *V. tahitensis* vanilla beans

8 ounces vodka

1. Place the vanilla beans in the jar, cut or uncut depending on your preference.

2. Pour the vodka into the jar, making sure the beans are entirely submerged.

3. Seal the jar tightly and store it in a cool, dark place for up to 12 months.

After 12 Months

4. Taste test your extract. Refer to taste testing on page 64.

5. When ready to use, either remove the beans or leave them in if preferred, ensuring that they are cut or folded small enough to remain submerged in the alcohol.

Double-Fold Mexican Vanilla Extract

Makes about 8 ounces of extract | Extract time: 12 months | Jar size: 16 ounces or larger

Making a double-fold vanilla extract isn't much different than single fold. It's simply twice the amount of vanilla beans in the same amount of alcohol. So why is it important?

As discussed in previous chapters, the essence of extract making is maximizing the sweetness in the same volume of moisture. How much sweetness can we possibly pack into a single teaspoon of extract? A double-fold extract tries to answer that question by doubling the sweetness without doubling the moisture content.

Mexican vanilla beans are a perfect first double-fold extract for their inherent bold sweetness, spicy vanilla kick, and undertones of mocha and caramel.

2 ounces Mexican *V. planifolia* vanilla beans

8 ounces vodka

1. Cut the vanilla beans into small pieces or tie them in a knot. With double the amount of beans, this will help ensure they stay fully submerged in the alcohol. Add the beans to the jar.

2. Pour the vodka into the jar, making sure the spirit covers all the beans.

3. Seal the jar tightly and store it in a cool, dark place for up to 12 months.

After 12 Months

4. Taste test your extract. Refer to taste testing on page 64.

5. When ready to use, either remove the beans or leave them in if preferred, ensuring that they are cut or folded small enough to remain submerged in the alcohol.

"I want to live the rest of my life, however long or short, with as much sweetness as I can decently manage, loving all the people I love, and doing as much as I can of the work I still have to do." —Audre Lorde

Vanilla Bean Sweet Dream Extract

Makes about 8 ounces of extract | Extract time: 12 months | Jar size: 8 ounces or larger

The use of Mexican and Indian vanilla beans within this recipe provides spicy mocha undertones with rummy notes of sweet molasses. It can be used in both sweet and savory dishes. Add a splash to the holiday ham as it's baking. Use it in pumpkin-spiced baked goods. You can even add a teaspoon to your holiday coffee, cider, or hot toddy!

½ ounce Mexican *V. planifolia* vanilla beans

½ ounce Indian *V. planifolia* vanilla beans

1 whole nutmeg

1 Ceylon cinnamon stick (Cassia cinnamon will also work)

1 teaspoon whole allspice berries

8 ounces 70–100 proof vodka

1. Slice the vanilla beans lengthwise or leave them whole if desired, and place them in the jar.
2. Place the nutmeg on a cutting board and cover with a dish towel. Using a kitchen mallet, break the nutmeg into 4–7 small pieces, then add the nutmeg pieces to the jar.
3. Break the cinnamon stick in half and add both halves to the jar. Add the allspice berries to the jar, then pour the vodka over all the ingredients, making sure everything is fully submerged in the spirit.
4. Seal the jar tightly and store it in a cool, dark place for 1 month.

After 1 Month

5. Remove both halves of the cinnamon stick.
6. Seal the jar tightly and store for 3 months.

After 4 Months

7. Remove the nutmeg and allspice berries by pouring the extract through a strainer or coffee filter. Return the extract and the vanilla beans to the jar.
8. Seal the jar tightly and store for another 8 months.

After 12 Months

9. Taste test your extract. Refer to taste testing on page 64.
10. When ready to use, either remove the beans or leave them in if preferred, ensuring that they are cut or folded small enough to remain submerged in the alcohol.

1/2 Tbsp/7.5ml

Indonesian Dark Rum Delight

Makes about 8 ounces of extract | Extract time: 18 months | Jar size: 8 ounces or larger

Dark rum produces a taste that is entirely unique. Many dark rums are matured in oak casks that were previously used for bourbon. So the sweetness of the rum is complemented by subtle hints of smoky and sweet bourbon. The marriage of the two flavors can be a beautiful new extract taste when paired with the right vanilla bean, which typically requires trial and error.

To help speed the process along, we are going to share one of our favorite dark-rum vanilla extracts that can be used in rich creams, dark chocolates, frostings, brownies, and more.

1 ounce Indonesian *V. planifolia* vanilla beans

8 ounces Zacapa Dark Rum (or your favorite dark rum)

1. Slice open each vanilla bean lengthwise to expose the caviar and help expedite extraction. Place the vanilla beans in the jar.

2. Pour the dark rum into the jar, making sure the beans are entirely submerged.

3. Seal the jar tightly and store it in a cool, dark place for up to 18 months. (That is not a typo. A good dark-spirit extract can require 6 additional months over regular extraction time for the richest extract experience.)

After 18 Months

4. Taste test your extract. Refer to taste testing on page 64.

5. When ready to use, either remove the beans or leave them in if preferred, ensuring that they are cut or folded small enough to remain submerged in the alcohol.

Double-Fold Mexican Vanilla with Bourbon

Makes about 8 ounces of double-fold extract | Extract time: 18 months | Jar size: 16 ounces or larger

A nice bourbon is a wonderful spirit. Dark, sweet, smoky, and rich, bourbon contains flavor compounds that complement many types of baked goods. When extract makers begin to explore bourbon extracts for the first time, it can be a little overwhelming if they aren't already accustomed to the taste. The characteristics of bourbon are outlined in detail on page 37. We selected Woodford Reserve for this recipe because of its super sweet taste, soft hints of smoke, and caramel undertones.

Approach bourbon-based extracts cautiously, with vanilla beans that you are already familiar with. We recommend starting with a Mexican vanilla bean for its rich, spicy, smoky, and sweet undertones. When using bourbon, we also recommend making a double-fold extract, for twice the amount of vanilla sweetness to overcome the inherent smokiness of the spirit.

A bourbon extract is wonderful in rich desserts to add hints of caramel and honey and a soft touch of lemon. It can also be used on proteins: when you are searing a salmon or grilling chicken or steak, add a splash of bourbon vanilla extract. It's wonderful in barbecue and buffalo wing sauces as well.

2 ounces Mexican *V. planifolia* vanilla beans

8 ounces Woodford Reserve Straight Bourbon (or your favorite bourbon)

1. Cut the vanilla beans into small pieces or tie them in a knot. With double the amount of beans, this will help ensure they stay fully submerged in the alcohol. (Slicing may be preferred for first-time bourbon users to allow the vanilla taste to really shine through.) Add the beans to the jar.

2. Pour the bourbon into the jar, making sure the spirit covers all the beans.

3. Seal the jar tightly and store it in a cool, dark place for at least 12 months. Bourbons and dark rums often require up to 18 months before they are entirely ready.

After 12-18 Months

4. Taste test your extract. Refer to taste testing on page 64.

5. When ready to use, either remove the beans or leave them in if preferred, ensuring that they are cut or folded small enough to remain submerged in the alcohol.

The
KRAKEN
BLACK SPICED
RUM
The
KRAKEN
BLACK SPICED
RUM
94
PROOF

Spiced Rum Double-Fold Blend

Makes about 8 ounces of extract | Extract time: 12 months | Jar size: 16 ounces or larger

When we first expanded our extract horizons beyond vanilla beans and traditional spirits, this was the first novelty extract we made. Homemade extracting usually begins with basic bourbon, vodka, and rum. When you get the hang of it after a year or so, you begin to branch out, trying different beans and different spirits for different cooking applications.

During the holiday season a few years ago, we made homemade eggnog with spiced rum, and we realized that spiced rum would be perfect in just about everything we make during the holiday season. Pumpkin-spiced cookies, gingerbread, pumpkin pies, mincemeat, apple pecan pies, and, of course, eggnog and so much more. So why not make a vanilla extract with spiced rum?

Typically, we don't encourage making extracts with spirits that contain artificial flavors. For example, a vanilla-flavored vodka does not result in double the vanilla taste if used for extract making. In fact, the taste is metallic and somewhat medicinal. We often get the same poor results with fruit-flavored spirits. They just don't turn out well. However, the taste of spiced rum is the clear exception to the rule, and it is wonderful for DIY vanilla extract.

1 ounce Papua New Guinea *V. tahitensis* vanilla beans, or another fruity, spicy vanilla bean

1 ounce Madagascar vanilla beans, or another classic, buttery vanilla bean

8 ounces Kraken Black Spiced Rum

1. Cut the vanilla beans into small pieces or tie them in a knot. With double the amount of beans, this will help ensure they stay fully submerged in the alcohol. Add the beans to the jar.

2. Pour the spiced rum into the jar, making sure the spirit covers all the beans.

3. Seal the jar tightly and store it in a cool, dark place for 12 months.

After 12 Months

4. Taste test your extract. Refer to taste testing on page 64.

5. When ready to use, either remove the beans or leave them in if preferred, ensuring that they are cut or folded small enough to remain submerged in the alcohol.

Sous Vide Vanilla Extract: An Option for Faster Extraction

Makes about 8 ounces of extract | Extract time: 3 months | Jar size: 8 ounces or larger

One of the great challenges of extract making at home is the time required to make the extract. There are very few things that you do in your kitchen that require an entire year. There is a shortcut option that utilizes a kitchen tool called a sous vide. This recipe was inspired by one of our extract-making friends, Mr. Gingrich.

A sous vide is a small appliance that sits on the edge of a large container or cooking pot filled with water. It circulates and heats the water inside the pot over extended periods of time. In extract making, the ability to apply low heat to your extract jars can effectively speed up extraction. In fact, when using a sous vide, your extract can be ready in as little as 3 months. It does alter the taste slightly. The use of heat in extract making can negatively impact many of the three hundred flavor compounds in vanilla beans. However, many people love and use this method regularly. Others prefer the natural taste of an extract derived without heating. We recommend Madagascar vanilla beans because their taste will be familiar to you, making it easier to recognize the impact of the sous vide on the finished extract taste.

1 ounce Madagascar *V. planifolia* vanilla beans

8 ounces of your favorite spirit (we have had success with bourbon and vodka)

1. Fill a large pot with water, so the water level is equal to or higher than the height of your 8-ounce jar.

2. Attach the sous vide to the cooking pot or water container according to the manufacturer's instructions. Set the sous vide to 135°F.

3. Slice your vanilla beans lengthwise, exposing the caviar for expedited sweetness, then place them in your jar.

4. Pour the spirit into the jar, making sure the beans are entirely submerged.

5. Seal the jar tightly, place it in the water container, and start the timer for 96 hours.

6. Monitor your pot of water, as the heated water will evaporate. Most sous vide units will shut down if the water level drops below a critical point, so you will need to add more hot

water at least once daily. We recommend doing this right before you go to bed, so the sous vide doesn't turn off due to a low water level while you are sleeping.

7. After 96 hours, remove your jar from the pot of water.

8. Open the extract jar and conduct a taste test immediately. Refer to taste testing on page 64.

9. Check the jar monthly for taste. As soon as you like the taste, the extract can be used. If you are tasting too much alcohol and not enough vanilla, then wait another month and test again. When you believe your extract is ready, either remove the beans or leave them in if preferred, ensuring that they are cut or folded small enough to remain submerged in the alcohol.

"Desserts are the fairy tales of the kitchen—
a happily-ever-after to supper."
—Terri Guillemets

Chocolate, Caramel, and Coffee Extracts

Salted Caramel Vanilla Extract

Makes about 8 ounces of extract | Extract time: 12 months | Jar size: 32 ounces (1 quart)

This extract treat has become one of the most popular concoctions that our extract-making pros make and use often during the holidays. It's a great example of an extract and an emulsion in a single recipe. It's a perfect extract for brownies, caramels, fudge, and so much more. It's even great in your morning coffee or in milkshakes!

1 ounce Tanzanian *V. planifolia* grade A vanilla beans

5 ounces caramel squares (approximately 15 pieces)

½ teaspoon sea salt

8 ounces vodka

1. Slice the vanilla beans lengthwise and then cut each bean in half to maximize vanilla flavor. Place the beans in the jar.

2. Add the caramel squares and sea salt, then pour the vodka into the jar, making sure all ingredients are entirely submerged.

3. Seal the lid tightly on the jar, give it a gentle shake, and store it in a cool, dark place for 2 months. The caramel pieces will dissolve within a few days inside of the spirit.

After 2 Months

4. Pour the extract through a coffee filter to remove the larger remaining portions of the dissolved caramel. Return the extract to the jar with the vanilla beans and continue storing for 4–10 more months. Given the emulsion of caramel in this recipe, it can be ready to use in as little as 6 months based on your taste preferences, but we recommend waiting 12 months.

After 12 Months

5. Taste test your extract. Refer to taste testing on page 64.

6. If you're satisfied with the flavor, remove the vanilla beans and begin using your extract.

"A cup brimful of sweetness cannot spill even one drop of bitter water, no matter how suddenly jarred." —Amy Carmichael

Chocolate and Vanilla Extract

Makes about 8 ounces of extract | Extract time: 12 months | Jar size: 16 ounces or larger

Experience a familiar taste and aroma with this rich and creamy extract that blends the world's two favorite flavors: chocolate and vanilla. Did you know that chocolate has just as much variation in taste as vanilla depending on the region where it is grown? This finished extract can be used to replace vanilla extract in any chocolate recipe, or it can be used to add a hint of chocolate to recipes that traditionally call for vanilla. Sri Lankan vanilla beans, with their natural notes of dark chocolate, pair exceptionally well with cacao for this sweet extract.

1 ounce Sri Lankan *V. planifolia* vanilla beans

1 cup roasted cacao nibs

8 ounces white rum or vodka, plus more if needed

Note: Do not throw away your used cacao nibs. You can dry and powder them for use in baking or as a garnish on cakes and other desserts.

1. Slice the vanilla beans lengthwise and then cut each bean in half to maximize vanilla flavor. Place the beans in the jar.

2. Add the cacao nibs to the jar, then pour the white rum or vodka over the ingredients. The cacao nibs may float, and that is OK.

3. Seal the lid tightly on the jar and store it in a cool, dark place for 3 months.

After 3 Months

4. Taste test your extract. Refer to taste testing on page 64. If the presence of the chocolate is satisfactory to your liking, then remove the cacao nibs (see recipe note) by pouring the extract through a strainer. (If you prefer a richer chocolate taste, you can let the nibs extract for another 3 months and taste test again.)

5. Return the vanilla beans and extract to the jar. The cacao will have absorbed some of the alcohol, so top off the alcohol to the original fluid line after removing the cacao. Reseal the jar and store for another 9 months.

After 12 Months

6. Taste test again to ensure it is to your liking. If you're satisfied with the flavor, remove the vanilla beans and begin using your extract.

Captain

Coffee Bean Cinnamon Spice Extract

Makes about 8 ounces of extract | Extract time: 3 months | Jar size: 16 ounces or larger

This extract captures the taste of a warm cup of coffee with a soft hint of vanilla and cinnamon. Now, concentrate that taste into a jar of extract that can be added to any of your favorite drinks or sweet baking treats for added flavor depth and richness. Put a couple drops in your morning cup of coffee for enhanced sweetness.

In this case, the vanilla beans are used as a flavor enhancer, not to be fully extracted, so the beans are listed by quantity rather than by weight.

2–3 Indonesian *V. planifolia* vanilla beans

1 Ceylon cinnamon stick

1 cup medium-roast whole coffee beans

8 ounces vodka

1. Slice the vanilla beans lengthwise, cut them in half, and add them to the jar. This extract emphasizes the coffee and cinnamon, and vanilla is the binder. As such, cutting the vanilla beans here to maximize flavor in a short period of time is preferred.

2. Break the cinnamon stick in half and add it to the jar.

3. Using a mortar and pestle, break and grind the coffee beans, then add them to the jar.

4. Pour the vodka over all ingredients in the jar. Note that the coffee beans will float, and that is OK.

5. Seal the jar tightly and store in a cool, dark place for 2 months.

After 2 Months

6. Pour the extract through a coffee filter to remove the coffee beans and cinnamon stick.

7. Return the extract and vanilla beans to the jar. Reseal the jar and store in a cool, dark place for 1 more month.

After 3 Months

8. Taste test your extract. Refer to taste testing on page 64. If you're satisfied with the flavor, remove the vanilla beans and begin using your extract.

Mocha Vanilla Extract

Makes about 8 ounces of extract | Extract time: 12 months | Jar size: 16 ounces or larger

This sweet and creative extract was originally inspired by one of our favorite extract-making friends, Starlette. The extract is exactly how it sounds. It's that wonderful coffee, vanilla, and chocolate flavor that we all recognize as mocha. Use this extract in coffee cakes, brownies, or cookies. Like most extracts, it's also a great addition to hot chocolate, your favorite lattes, or iced mochas.

½ ounce Madagascar *V. planifolia* vanilla beans

½ ounce Mexican *V. planifolia* vanilla beans

½ cup dark Arabica coffee beans (or your favorite coffee bean)

½ cup roasted cacao nibs

8 ounces vodka, plus more as needed

1. Place whole vanilla beans (tied or bent) in the jar without slicing them to keep the caviar inside the pods during extraction.

2. Using a mortar and pestle, crack the coffee beans, then add them to the jar. Note: Do *not* grind them down to a powder—simply crack them.

3. Add the cacao nibs to the jar, then pour the vodka over the ingredients. The coffee beans may float, and that is OK. Remember that all the ingredients will displace the liquid, which is why you should begin with a larger jar.

4. Seal the jar and store in a cool, dark place for 1 month.

After 1 Month

5. Remove the cacao nibs and coffee beans by pouring the extract through a strainer or coffee filter.

6. Return the vanilla beans and extract to the jar. The coffee beans and cacao nibs will have absorbed some of the alcohol, so top off the jar with your spirit to the original fluid line. Reseal the jar and store in a cool, dark place for 11 more months.

After 12 Months

7. Taste test your extract. Refer to taste testing on page 64. If you're satisfied with the flavor, remove the vanilla beans and begin using your extract.

Fruit Extracts

Strawberry Vanilla Extract

Makes about 8 ounces of extract | Extract time: 1–2 months | Jar size: 12 ounces or larger

We begin our journey into fruit extracts with the natural sweetness of one of our favorite fruits: the strawberry. This is a must-have extract to add to your favorite teas, fruit-based desserts, smoothies, vinaigrettes, and more. It's easy to make and adds a flavor burst of sweetness to your cooking. Adding vanilla beans to this (or any) recipe creates a creamier, smoother extract that binds the flavors of the spirit and the strawberry together. One ounce of dried strawberries can also be used with a 70–100 proof spirit instead of Everclear.

8–12 ounces fresh strawberries

2 Tahitian *V. tahitensis* vanilla beans

8 ounces 195 proof Everclear

1. Wash 8 ounces of strawberries, cut them into small pieces, and place them in the jar.
2. Split the vanilla beans lengthwise, cut them in half, then add them to jar.
3. Pour the Everclear into the jar. Make sure all ingredients are entirely submerged.
4. Close the jar and store it in a cool, dark place for 1 month.

After 1 Month

5. Pour the extract through a strainer to remove and discard the strawberry pieces.
6. Taste test your extract. Refer to taste testing on page 64.
7. If you would like a more pronounced strawberry flavor, return your extract and vanilla beans to the jar, add 4 ounces of fresh strawberries to your extract, seal the jar, and store it for 1 more month.

After 2 Months

8. Pour the extract through a strainer to remove and discard the strawberry pieces. Your extract is now finished.
9. Remove the vanilla beans, or leave them in for added sweetness over time if preferred, ensuring that they are cut small enough to remain submerged in the alcohol.

Caramel Apple Vanilla Extract

Makes about 8 ounces of extract | Extract time: 6 months | Jar size: 32 ounces (1 quart)

Apples are fall leaves, crisp morning air, and warm apple pie. They are one of the sweet flavors that fill our kitchen with early signs of the upcoming holiday season. Capturing the pure essence of sweet apples is the goal of this extract. It is the perfect addition to baked goods, hot apple cider, apple pie, and much, much more during the holiday cooking season. We make this recipe even sweeter with the addition of caramel, which evokes memories of the sweet taste of caramel apples in the fall.

½ cup dried apple slices (×2)

½ ounce Papua New Guinea *V. tahitensis* vanilla beans

5 ounces caramel squares (approximately 15 squares)

8 ounces vodka

1. Place ½ cup of the dried apples in the jar.

2. Slice the vanilla beans lengthwise and cut them in half. Add the vanilla and the caramel pieces to the jar on top of the apples.

3. Pour the vodka over the ingredients in the jar. The apples may float on top of the vodka, and that is OK. They will still extract, but keeping them submerged is preferable, as it increases the amount of surface area for extraction. If the vanilla beans and caramel don't hold the apples down to the bottom of the jar, a glass fermentation weight can be added on top of the ingredients if you are using a mason jar.

4. Seal the jar and store it in a cool, dark place for 2 months. The caramel pieces will dissolve within a few days inside of the spirit.

After 2 Months

5. Pour the extract through a coffee filter to remove the apples (see recipe note) and the larger remaining portions of the dissolved caramel. Return the extract and the vanilla beans to the jar.

6. Add ½ cup of new dried apple slices. Seal the jar and store for 2 months.

After 4 Months

7. Remove the apples again, leaving just the vanilla beans and the extract. Seal the jar and store for 2 months.

Note: The used apple slices can be dried and then baked at 150°F for 10–20 minutes for crispy apple chips.

After 6 Months

8. Taste test your extract. Refer to taste testing on page 64.

9. When ready to use, leave the vanilla beans in the jar or remove them depending on your preference. Be careful to keep them submerged by folding or cutting the beans as necessary.

"Good apple pies are a considerable part of our domestic happiness." —Jane Austen

Banana Vanilla Bean Extract

Makes about 8 ounces of extract | Extract time: 3 months | Jar size: 12 ounces or larger

For banana breads, banana cream pie, bananas Foster, or any other banana-based dessert, a simple banana extract will enhance the sweetness and add a familiar taste that we all know and love. Of course, this sweet banana treat can also be added to your favorite smoothies, fillings, and much more. Add a single vanilla bean to this extract to softly blend the banana and the spirit into a sweet and creamy banana concentration. Given the naturally bland taste of bananas, at least three rounds of extraction are required to yield the desired flavor concentration in this extract.

1 ounce dried, unsweetened banana chips (×3) that contain no added sugar or oil

1 large Peruvian *V. pompona* or Mexican *V. pompona* vanilla bean

8 ounces vodka

"The pursuit of perfection, then, is the pursuit of sweetness." —Matthew Arnold

1. Place 1 ounce banana chips in the jar.

2. Slice the vanilla bean lengthwise, cut it in half, then add it to the jar.

3. Pour the vodka over the ingredients in the jar. Make sure the vanilla is fully submerged. The banana chips may float and that is OK.

4. Seal the lid tightly and store in a cool, dark place for 1 month.

After 1 Month

5. Remove the banana chips (see recipe note) by pouring the extract through a strainer, pressing gently on the banana chips to squeeze any absorbed alcohol back into the extract. Return the extract and vanilla bean to the jar and add 1 ounce of new dried banana chips. Top off the alcohol if needed.

6. Seal the lid and store the jar in a cool, dark place for 1 month.

After 2 Months

7. Remove the banana chips by pouring the extract through a strainer. Return the extract and vanilla bean to the jar.

8. Add 1 ounce of new dried banana chips, reseal the jar, and store it in a cool, dark place for 1 more month.

After 3 Months

9. Remove the banana chips by pouring the extract through a strainer.

10. Taste test your extract. Refer to taste testing on page 64.

11. If you're not satisfied with the strength of the banana flavor, complete one more round of extraction with new dried banana chips, then remove the banana and vanilla before use.

> **Note:** You can dry the banana chips and then heat them in the oven for 10–20 minutes at 150°F for a crunchy banana chip snack.

Blueberry Vanilla Spice Extract

Makes about 8 ounces of extract | Extract time: 12 months | Jar size: 16 ounces or larger

We love blueberries for homemade pancakes, syrups and sweet yogurt toppings. This recipe was inspired by one of our extract-making friends, Michelle. While we are using fresh blueberries in this recipe, 1 ounce of dried blueberries can also be used with a 70–100 proof spirit instead of Everclear.

1 ounce Tahitian *V. tahitensis* vanilla beans

1 Ceylon cinnamon stick

8–12 ounces fresh blueberries

8 ounces 195 proof Everclear

Note: You can begin using this extract in 2 months for the taste of the blueberries and cinnamon, but for the full taste of the vanilla we recommend waiting 12 months.

1. Slice the vanilla beans lengthwise, cut them in half, then place them in the jar.

2. Break the cinnamon stick in half and add both halves to the jar, then add 8 ounces of fresh blueberries.

3. Pour the Everclear into the jar, making sure that all ingredients are fully submerged.

4. Seal the jar tightly and store it in a cool, dark place for 1 month.

After 1 Month

5. Remove the blueberries and the cinnamon by pouring the extract through a strainer or coffee filter, pressing the absorbed alcohol out of the blueberries and into the jar. Return the extract and the vanilla beans to the jar.

6. Taste test your extract. Refer to taste testing on page 64. If you would like a more pronounced blueberry flavor, add 4 ounces of fresh blueberries to your extract and store for 1 more month. After the additional month, remove the blueberries and continue to extract the vanilla for 10 more months.

After 12 Months

7. Taste test your extract. If you like the taste, remove the vanilla beans from the jar and begin using your extract. If not, continue to store and taste test at 1-month intervals.

Cherry Vanilla Extract

Makes about 8 ounces of extract | Extract time: 12 months | Jar size: 16 ounces or larger

Homemade cherry extract is a sweet treat without a lot of effort. Cherry extract can be used in beverages, frostings, fruit creams, and so much more to sweeten the fruity notes of many desserts. It's a great way to have the wonderful flavor of cherries available even when cherries are not in season. While we are using fresh cherries in this recipe, 1 ounce of dried cherries can also be used with a 70–100 proof spirit instead of Everclear.

1 ounce Tongan *V. planifolia* vanilla beans

8–12 ounces fresh cherries, pitted

8 ounces 195 proof Everclear

1. Slice the vanilla beans lengthwise, cut them in half, and place them in the jar.

2. Add 8 ounces of cherries to the jar.

3. Pour the Everclear into the jar, making sure all ingredients are fully submerged.

4. Seal the jar tightly and store in a cool, dark place for 1 month.

After 1 Month

5. Remove the cherries by pouring the extract through a strainer or coffee filter. Return the extract and the vanilla beans to the jar.

6. Taste test your extract. Refer to taste testing on page 64. If you would like a more pronounced cherry flavor, add 4 ounces of fresh cherries to your extract and store for 1 more month. After the additional month, remove the cherries and continue to extract the vanilla for 10 more months.

After 12 Months

7. Taste test the extract. If you like the taste, remove the vanilla beans from the jar and begin using your extract. If not, continue to store and taste test at 1-month intervals.

Creamy Coconut Vanilla Extract

Makes about 8 ounces of extract | Extract time: 1 month | Jar size: 12 ounces or larger

Homemade coconut extract is so easy to make and adds a sweet and tropical coconut flavor to all your favorite recipes. Coconut extract is especially good when used in making macaroons, lemon bars, meringue, coconut cream, and much more. The addition of a single vanilla bean in this sweet extract will bind the coconut and the spirit into a creamy, rich, concentrated flavor. Hawaiian or Mexican *V. pompona* vanilla beans are a perfect match for this application.

1 cup shredded unsweetened coconut

1–2 Hawaiian *V. planifolia* or 1–2 Mexican *V. pompona* vanilla beans

8 ounces white rum

Note: For a slightly different outcome, toast the coconut for 10 minutes at 150°F before adding it to the extract. The toasted coconut will add nutty and sweet undertones.

1. Place the shredded coconut in the jar.

2. Cut the vanilla bean into 2 or 3 pieces and place them on top of the coconut in the jar.

3. Pour in the rum, ensuring that the coconut and vanilla are fully submerged.

4. Seal the jar and store it in a cool, dark place for 1 month. Shake once or twice weekly. You will notice that the coconut will begin to turn brown due to the vanilla bean oils. That is OK.

After 1 Month

5. Taste test your extract. Refer to taste testing on page 64. If the coconut is not as strong as you would like, you can store the extract for an additional 1 month, shaking the jar once or twice weekly.

6. When ready to use, strain the extract by pouring it through a strainer or a coffee filter, pressing the coconut to squeeze the absorbed alcohol back into the extract. Discard the coconut. Remove the vanilla bean, or leave it in for added sweetness over time if preferred, ensuring that it is cut or folded small enough to remain submerged in the alcohol.

Cranberry Vanilla Orange Extract

Makes about 8 ounces of extract | Extract time: 6–12 months | Jar size: 32 ounces (1 quart)

This extract is more complex and entirely worth the added effort. It's a beautiful, festive, and sweet finished extract that will enhance the sweet taste of virtually anything you cook with it. For tarts, creams, sauces, holiday cookies, breads, and even splashed in a beverage, this is a wonderful extract to have in your kitchen year-round. It's especially good in holiday hot wassail or a grown-up hot toddy.

1 ounce Cook Island *V. tahitensis* vanilla beans

3 medium oranges (×2)

2 ounces dried cranberries (×2)

1 teaspoon whole cloves

8 ounces dark rum with an alcohol content of 75–85 percent (150–170 proof), plus more as needed

1. Slice the vanilla beans lengthwise, cut them in half, and place them in the jar.

2. Slice 3 unpeeled oranges into pieces small enough to fit into the extract jar. Add the oranges, 2 ounces of dried cranberries, and the cloves to the jar.

3. Pour the rum over all the ingredients, ensuring everything is completely submerged. If you are using a mason jar, you can add a glass fermentation weight on top of your ingredients to keep them submerged.

4. Seal the jar and store it in a cool, dark place for 1 month.

After 1 Month

5. Pour all contents through a strainer, then remove and discard the oranges and the cranberries, gently pressing the fruit to squeeze the absorbed alcohol back into the extract. Return the extract, vanilla beans, and cloves to the jar.

6. Add 2 ounces of new dried cranberries and fresh orange peels from 3 oranges. Make sure the peel is carefully cleaned without any pith. (Do not add the entire orange slices this time, only the orange peel.)

7. Add more rum to cover the ingredients if necessary.

8. Seal the jar tightly and store in a cool, dark place for 1 month.

After 2 Months

9. Remove the orange peels, cranberries, and cloves by pouring the extract through a strainer.

10. Return the vanilla beans and extract to the jar, reseal it, and store it for 4–10 more months in a cool, dark place.

After 12 Months

11. Taste test your extract. Refer to taste testing on page 64. If you like the taste, you can begin using your extract. If not, continue to store and taste test at 1-month intervals.

12. When ready to use, remove the vanilla beans, or leave them in for added sweetness over time if preferred, ensuring that they are cut or folded small enough to remain submerged in the alcohol.

Grapefruit Extract

Makes about 8 ounces of extract | Extract time: 6 months | Jar size: 32 ounces (1 quart)

Grapefruit is one of our favorite citrus treats every winter. Paul had a Ruby Red grapefruit tree at his childhood home in Arizona and there was something magical about plucking that huge grapefruit from the branch, bringing it to the kitchen, cutting it open, sprinkling it with salt or sugar, and eating each juicy triangle one at a time. It's beautiful (especially the Ruby Reds), it's healthy, and it's a shame that it doesn't grow year-round! With this sweet extract, you can keep the taste of grapefruit in your cooking all the time. Try this extract in beverages, cakes, sorbets, fruit salads, salad dressings, and more.

1 ounce Tanzanian *V. planifolia* vanilla beans

1 large grapefruit (×3)

8 ounces 150–170 proof rum

Note: Use dried, leftover zest pieces to make grapefruit-flavored sugar. Simply add the dried zest to 1 cup of sugar in a bag, shake and let sit for 1–2 weeks, and enjoy!

1. Slice the vanilla beans lengthwise, cut them in half, and place them in the jar.

2. Slice the unpeeled grapefruit into pieces small enough to fit into the extract jar, then add them on top of the vanilla.

3. Pour the rum into the jar, ensuring that all ingredients are completely submerged. If you are using a mason jar, you can add a glass fermentation weight on top of your ingredients to keep them submerged.

4. Seal the jar and store it in a cool, dark place for 1 month.

After 1 Month

5. Remove and discard the grapefruit by pouring the contents through a strainer, gently pressing the fruit to squeeze the absorbed alcohol back into the extract. Return the extract and vanilla beans to the jar.

6. Zest the outer peel of 1 fresh grapefruit, avoiding zesting down into the white pith. Add the zested peel to the extract.

7. Reseal the jar and store it in a cool, dark place for 1 month.

After 2 Months

8. Remove the grapefruit zest (see recipe note) by pouring the contents through a fine mesh strainer. Return the extract and the vanilla to the jar.

9. Add the zest of the outer peel of 1 fresh grapefruit for a second time.

10. Reseal the jar and store for 1 month, shaking regularly.

After 3 Months

11. Remove the grapefruit zest by pouring the contents through a strainer. Return the extract and the vanilla to the jar.

12. Reseal the jar and store in a cool, dark place for 3 more months.

After 6 Months

13. Taste test the extract by smelling it for a high concentration of grapefruit or by dipping your finger into the extract and tasting it. The grapefruit taste will be strong and extremely concentrated. The taste of the grapefruit should be dominant, but the alcohol taste will still be present.

14. When ready to use, remove the vanilla beans, or leave them in for added sweetness over time if preferred, ensuring that they are cut or folded small enough to remain submerged in the alcohol.

Huckleberry Vanilla Extract

Makes about 8 ounces of extract | Extract time: 5 months | Jar size: 12 ounces or larger

Huckleberries are a late-summer treat. They are sweet, a little tart, and wonderful with pancakes, chocolate desserts, and other sweets. This extract recipe will allow you to incorporate huckleberries into your cooking year-round without the need for fresh huckleberries. It's easy to make and ready in (relatively) no time! The addition of vanilla beans softens and binds the tart taste of the extract with the smooth vodka. Vanilla beans from Vanuatu are ideal for this extract given their soft cinnamon undertones and fruity accents.

1 ounce Vanuatu *V. planifolia* vanilla beans

1 ounce dried huckleberries

8 ounces vodka

"Find the sweetness in your own heart, then you may find the sweetness in every heart."
—Rumi

1. Slice the vanilla beans lengthwise, cut them in half, and place them in the jar.

2. Add the dried huckleberries to the jar.

3. Pour the vodka over the ingredients, making sure everything is fully submerged.

4. Seal the jar and store it in a cool, dark place for 2 months.

After 2 Months

5. Pour the contents through a strainer to remove and discard the used huckleberries, gently pressing the fruit to squeeze the absorbed alcohol back into the extract. Return the extract and the vanilla beans to the jar.

6. Reseal the jar and store in a cool, dark place for 3 more months.

After 5 Months

7. Taste test your extract. Refer to taste testing on page 64. If you like the taste, you can begin using your extract. If not, continue to store and taste test at 1-month intervals.

8. When ready to use, remove the vanilla beans, or leave them in for added sweetness over time if preferred, ensuring that they are cut or folded small enough to remain submerged in the alcohol.

Lemon Vanilla Extract

Makes about 8 ounces of extract | Extract time: 1 month | Jar size: 16 ounces or larger

Lemon extract has universal use in cooking, mixology, and baking applications year-round. A proper lemon extract is highly concentrated—even more concentrated than pure lemon juice. This is important because it allows you to maximize the amount of lemon flavor in your cooking without the need to add additional fluid. Vanilla adds a creamy overture that binds the flavor of the lemons with the spirit for a smooth, sweet final extract.

10–20 medium lemons

2 Ecuadorian *V. tahitensis* vanilla beans

8 ounces vodka

1. Clean the outer peel of the lemons, then peel the rinds off, being careful not to include the white pith. Place the lemon peels in the jar.

2. Slice the vanilla beans lengthwise, cut them in half, and place them in the jar.

3. Pour the vodka over the ingredients in the jar. The lemon peels may float on top of the vodka, and that is OK. They will still extract, but keeping them submerged is preferable. To keep the lemon peels submerged, a glass fermentation weight can be added if you are using a mason jar.

4. Seal the jar and store it in a cool, dark place for 1 month.

After 1 Month

5. Remove the lemon peels by pouring your extract through a strainer.

6. Taste test the extract by smelling it for a high concentration of lemon or dipping your finger into the extract and tasting it. The lemon taste will be strong and extremely concentrated. The taste of the lemon should be dominant, but the alcohol taste will still be present. If a stronger lemon taste is desired, repeat the process one more time, adding fresh peels from 10 new lemons and storing the jar for 1 more month.

7. When ready to use, remove the vanilla beans, or leave them in for added sweetness over time if preferred, ensuring that they are cut or folded small enough to remain submerged in the alcohol.

"You can't touch love, but you can feel the sweetness that it pours into everything." —Anne Sullivan Macy

Orange Cacao Vanilla Extract

Makes about 8 ounces of extract | Extract time: 4 months | Jar size: 16 ounces or larger

Since making vanilla extract can take more than a year, many of our extract-making friends have found that they can make other extracts faster while they are waiting for their vanilla extract to be complete. This extract combines two of our favorite flavors into a highly concentrated, unique blend that is wonderful in most of your sweetest baked creations to add a new and rich taste. For cakes, brownies, chocolate frostings, and chocolate pies, this extract is a must-have flavor in your baking arsenal. And it's ready to use in just a few months.

3–6 medium oranges

½ cup ground and roasted cacao nibs

1 ounce Indonesian *V. tahitensis* vanilla beans

8 ounces 195 proof Everclear

1. Clean the outer peel of the oranges. Using a zester, zest 3–6 oranges to collect 2 tablespoons of peel, being careful not to include the white pith. Add the zest to the bottom of the jar, then add the cacao on top of the zest.

2. Cut 3 oranges into wedges and add them to the jar on top of the zest and cacao. If you are using a mason jar and have a glass fermentation weight, you can set it on top of the oranges to keep any ingredients from floating.

3. Add the vanilla beans, either whole or sliced, on top of the oranges and cacao.

4. Pour the Everclear into the jar, making sure all ingredients are fully submerged.

5. Seal the jar and store it in a cool, dark place for 1 month.

After 1 Month

6. Remove and discard the orange slices, gently pressing the fruit to squeeze the absorbed alcohol back into the extract. Keep the orange zest, cacao nibs, and vanilla beans submerged in the jar and continue to store for 3 more months.

After 4 Months

7. Taste test your extract. Refer to taste testing on page 64. If you like the taste, remove the cacao (see recipe note) and the zest by pouring the extract through a strainer or coffee filter,

"There is nothing better than a friend, unless it is a friend with chocolate."
—Linda Grayson

and begin using the extract. If you want a stronger cacao or orange flavor, add 2 tablespoons of fresh orange zest and/or fresh cacao and continue to store and taste test at 1-month intervals.

8. When ready to use, remove the vanilla beans, or leave them in for added sweetness over time if preferred, ensuring that they are cut or folded small enough to remain submerged in the alcohol.

Note: The cacao nibs can be dried and turned into a powder to be used in baking, coffee, and much more.

Orange and Vanilla Cream Extract

Makes about 8 ounces of extract | Extract time: 12 months | Jar size: 16 ounces or larger

When we think of vanilla and orange, we think of the classic orange Creamsicles we all had as children. An orange and vanilla extract can be used for homemade ice cream, summertime treats, orange rolls, sweet breads, and much more.

7 medium Cara Cara oranges

1 ounce Madagascar *V. planifolia* vanilla beans

8 ounces vodka

1. Thoroughly clean the outside of the oranges, then peel their rinds off, being careful not to include the white pith. Place the peels in the jar.

2. Slice open the vanilla beans lengthwise, cut them in half, and add them to the jar.

3. Pour the vodka into the jar, making sure the ingredients are fully submerged.

4. Seal the jar and store it in a cool, dark place for 2 months.

After 2 Months

5. Remove the orange peels by pouring the contents through a strainer. Return the extract and vanilla beans to the jar.

6. Taste test your extract. Refer to taste testing on page 64. If a stronger orange flavor is desired, repeat the process by adding peels from 7 fresh oranges and storing for 2 more months. After the additional 2 months, remove the orange peels and continue to extract the vanilla for 8 more months in a cool, dark place.

After 12 Months

7. Taste test your extract again. If you like the taste, begin using your extract. If not, continue to store and taste test at 1-month intervals.

8. When ready to use, remove the vanilla beans, or leave them in for added sweetness over time if preferred, ensuring that they are cut or folded small enough to remain submerged in the alcohol.

GREY

Peach Vanilla Extract

Makes about 8 ounces of extract | Extract time: 2 months | Jar size: 32 ounces (1 quart)

Is there anything that you can't extract? We don't think so, and this extract may top all the fruit extracts you have previously made. Who doesn't love the sweet taste of peaches? You can use peach extract to add that natural peachy sweetness to ice cream, smoothies, custards, and trifles. You can also make a refreshing and fruity peach iced tea or use it in sauces for chicken, seafood, and pork. Best of all, it isn't difficult to make. As with other fruit extracts, the vanilla beans are added as a binder and don't necessarily require a full year of extraction.

3 medium peaches (+1 ½ peaches after 1 month)

½ ounce Hawaiian *V. planifolia* vanilla beans

8 ounces 195 proof Everclear

1. Remove and discard the pit and the outer skin of 3 peaches, then slice the peaches and place them in the jar.

2. Leave the vanilla beans whole, or slice lengthwise and cut them in half, then add them to the jar.

3. Place a glass fermentation weight over the ingredients to ensure that the peaches stay submerged in the spirit, then pour the Everclear into the jar.

4. Seal the jar tightly and store in a cool, dark place for 1 month. The color of the peaches will turn from their bright, natural hue to a dark color.

After 1 Month

5. Pour the extract through a strainer to remove and discard the peaches, gently pressing the fruit to squeeze the absorbed alcohol back into the extract. Return the extract and the vanilla to the jar.

6. Add 1 ½ more fresh peaches (sliced, with the skin and pits removed) to the jar, then seal it and store for 1 more month.

After 2 Months

7. Remove and discard the peach slices by pouring the extract through a strainer or coffee filter. Return the extract and the vanilla beans to the jar. Your extract is now ready.

8. Either remove the vanilla beans or leave them in for added sweetness over time, ensuring that they are cut or folded small enough to remain submerged in the alcohol.

Peach and Caramel Vanilla Extract

Makes about 8 ounces of extract | Extract time: 6–8 months | Jar size: 32 ounces (1 quart)

This sweet extract can be used in syrups, ice cream toppings, and peach pies (of course!). It's a must-have specialty extract to add to your baking tool chest. Its extended extract time of up to 8 months allows the taste of the Comoros vanilla beans (or another vanilla bean of your choice) to shine through.

3 medium peaches (+1 ½ peaches after 1 month)

1 ounce Comoros *V. planifolia* vanilla beans

5 ounces (approximately 15 pieces) caramel squares

8 ounces 195 proof Everclear

1. Remove and discard the pit and the outer skin of 3 peaches, then slice the peaches and place them in the jar.

2. Slice the vanilla beans lengthwise, or leave them whole, cut them in half, and add them to the jar along with the caramel squares.

3. Pour the Everclear over all the ingredients in the jar, making sure everything is fully submerged.

4. Seal the jar and store it in a cool, dark place for 1 month. The color of the peaches will turn from their bright, natural hue to a dark color and the caramel squares will look coagulated, but don't worry, as this is normal.

After 1 Month

5. Pour the extract through a coffee filter to remove and discard the remnants of the dissolved caramel squares and the peaches, gently pressing the fruit to squeeze the absorbed alcohol back into the extract. Return the extract and the vanilla to the jar.

6. Add 1 ½ more fresh peaches (sliced, with the skin and pits removed) to the jar, then seal it and store for 1 month.

After 2 Months

7. Remove and discard the peaches by straining the contents, then return the extract and vanilla to the jar. Reseal the jar and store for 4 more months.

After 6 Months

8. Taste test your extract. Refer to taste testing on page 64. If you would like more vanilla taste, continue to store and taste test at 1-month intervals.

Peach Spice Extract

Makes about 8 ounces of extract | Extract time: 6–8 months | Jar size: 32 ounces (1 quart)

With applications in peach pie, tea, ice cream, peach cream, caramel sauce, cobbler, pie, coffee cake, muffins, biscotti, and sweet bread, this is an extract that you want in your kitchen cabinet all year-round. The extract time is 6–8 months to allow additional time for the Mexican vanilla bean, with its spicy undertones, to be further extracted.

3 medium peaches (+1 ½ peaches after 1 month)

1 Ceylon cinnamon stick (×2)

1 ounce Mexican *V. planifolia* vanilla beans

8 ounces 160 proof spiced rum

1. Remove and discard the outer skin and the pits of 3 peaches, then slice the peaches and place them in the jar.
2. Break the cinnamon stick in half and add it to the jar.
3. Slice the vanilla beans lengthwise, cut them in half, and add them to the jar.
4. Pour the spiced rum into the jar, making sure all the ingredients are fully submerged.
5. Seal the jar and store it in a cool, dark place for 1 month. The color of the peaches will turn from their bright, natural hue to a dark color.

After 1 Month

6. Pour the extract through a strainer to remove and discard the peaches and cinnamon, gently pressing the fruit to squeeze the absorbed alcohol back into the extract. Return the extract and the vanilla to the jar.
7. Add 1 ½ more fresh peaches (sliced, with the skin and pits removed) and a new cinnamon stick (broken in half) to the jar, then seal it and store for 1 month.

After 2 Months

8. Remove and discard the peaches and the cinnamon as you did at 1 month, returning the extract and the vanilla to the jar.
9. Reseal the jar and store it for 4 more months.

After 6 Months

10. Taste test your extract. Refer to taste testing on page 64. If you would like more vanilla present in the final taste, then allow the extract to sit with the vanilla beans for another 2 months.

Pineapple Paradise Vanilla Extract

Makes about 8 ounces of extract | Extract time: 2 months or more | Jar size: 16 ounces or larger

This extract is a little tart, but very sweet and intended to be used liberally year-round. For the fall and winter months, try adding a little to your holiday ham or cocktails and punches. This would also be lovely in a pineapple upside down cake. It's amazing in sorbets, creams, fruit salads, and even splashed over mahi-mahi on the grill.

1 ounce freeze-dried pineapple (×2)

1 ounce Hawaiian *V. planifolia* vanilla beans

8 ounces Hawaiian rum

1. Place the pineapple in the jar. You may need to break it into smaller pieces to make it fit.
2. Slice the vanilla beans lengthwise, cut them in half, and add them to the jar.
3. Pour the rum over the pineapple and vanilla, making sure all ingredients are fully submerged.
4. Seal the jar and store it in a cool, dark place for 1 month. The color of the pineapple will turn from its bright, natural hue to a dark color.

After 1 Month

5. Remove and discard the pineapple by pouring the contents through a strainer, gently pressing the fruit to squeeze the absorbed alcohol back into the extract. Return the extract and the vanilla to the jar.
6. Add 1 ounce of new freeze-dried pineapple to the extract.
7. Seal the jar and store it in a cool, dark place for 1 more month.

After 2 Months

8. Remove and discard the pineapple again, then return the extract and the vanilla to the jar.
9. Taste test your extract. Refer to taste testing on page 64.
10. If you would prefer a stronger vanilla presence, store the extract for up to an additional 6 months to allow the vanilla beans to extract further. You can also continue to replace the freeze-dried pineapple every month to enhance the pineapple taste concentration.

"Be like a pineapple: stand tall, wear a crown, and be sweet on the inside." —Katherine Gaskin

Raspberry Vanilla Extract

Makes about 8 ounces of extract | Extract time: 1 month | Jar size: 12 ounces or larger

Here's another simple extract with one of our favorite fruits: raspberries. This is a must-have extract to add to your favorite teas, fruit-based desserts, sorbets, smoothies, vinaigrettes, and more. When made correctly, raspberry extracts can add a flavor burst of sweetness to your cooking. While this recipe calls for fresh raspberries, 1 ounce of dried raspberries paired with 70 proof vodka can also be used.

8–12 ounces fresh raspberries

1–2 Tongan *V. planifolia* vanilla beans

8 ounces 195 proof Everclear

1. Place 8 ounces of raspberries in the jar.

2. Slice the vanilla beans lengthwise, cut them in half, and add them to the jar.

3. Pour the Everclear over the ingredients. The raspberries will float at first and begin to sink as they take on water. That is normal.

4. Seal the jar, shake it gently, and store it in a cool, dark place for 1 month.

After 1 Month

5. Pour the extract through a strainer to remove and discard the raspberry pieces, gently pressing the fruit to squeeze the absorbed alcohol back into the extract. Return the extract and vanilla to the jar.

6. Taste test your extract. Refer to taste testing on page 64. If you like the taste, then your extract is finished and you can begin using it.

7. If you would like a more pronounced raspberry flavor, add 4 ounces of fresh raspberries, reseal the jar, and store it for 1 month more month, then strain and discard the raspberry pieces as before.

8. When ready to use, keep the vanilla beans in the extract for added sweetness, ensuring that they are cut or folded small enough to remain submerged in the alcohol.

"Sometimes I'm so sweet even I can't stand it."
—Julie Andrews

Nut and Spice Extracts

Tito's
VODKA
25

Almond Vanilla Extract

Makes about 8 ounces of extract | Extract time: 2–3 months | Jar size: 12 ounces or larger

Almond extract is used to flavor amaretto, marzipan, cherry pie, homemade cookies, creams, frostings, and more. Surprisingly, the primary ingredient of our favorite almond extract is not almonds—it's apricot kernels! Apricot kernels are the small seeds inside the pit of an apricot that look almost identical to an almond. Like almonds, apricot kernels come in both a bitter and a sweet form, and both taste surprisingly like almonds, but sweeter and lighter.

Apricot kernels can be found online, so there is no need to purchase fresh apricots, remove the pits, crack the shells, and harvest the seed yourself. However, extract makers that have surplus apricots can harvest the seeds from the apricot pits at home if desired.

½ cup sweet apricot kernels

1–2 Madagascar *V. planifolia* vanilla beans

8 ounces vodka

1. Wash and dry the apricot kernels and place them in the jar.

2. Cut the vanilla beans into 2–4 pieces and add them to the jar.

3. Pour the vodka over the ingredients, ensuring everything is fully submerged.

4. Seal the jar and store it in a cool, dark place, shaking the jar occasionally. Homemade almond extract is ready for use after just 2–3 months.

After 2–3 Months

5. Taste test your extract. Refer to taste testing on page 64. The taste should be sweet with a hint of almond. However, it's reminiscent of vanilla extract and made in a fraction of the time.

6. When ready for use, pour the contents of the jar through a strainer or coffee filter, so only the liquid remains.

Note: The apricot kernels will absorb some of the spirit, so your final extract volume may be slightly less than the 8 ounces you began with. Also, when using apricot kernels, the question of toxicity sometimes arises within our online groups. To be safe, we never recommend consuming the pits on their own in large quantities.

"That's what dessert means to me: a dollop of sweet love in an otherwise cold world."
—Sarah Strohmeyer

Almond Chocolate Coconut Extract

Makes about 8 ounces of extract | Extract time: 4 months | Jar size: 16 ounces or larger

This sweet, fun, and indulgent recipe was inspired by our extract-making friend Lori. Use this extract in cookies, cakes, cannoli, chocolate cream pies, chocolate fudge, and more. Like the almond extract, we use apricot kernels in place of almonds for the same great almond taste but with enhanced sweetness.

½ cup shredded unsweetened coconut

½ cup roasted cacao nibs

⅛ cup sweet apricot kernels

1 ounce Madagascar *V. planifolia* vanilla beans

8 ounces vodka

1. Place the coconut in the jar, then add the cacao nibs.
2. Wash and dry the apricot kernels and add them to the jar on top of the coconut and cacao.
3. Slice the vanilla beans lengthwise, cut them in half, and add them to the jar last.
4. Pour the vodka over all the ingredients, ensuring everything is fully submerged.
5. Seal the jar and store it in a cool, dark place, shaking it occasionally, for 4 months.

After 4 Months

6. Remove the cacao nibs, coconut, and apricot kernels by pouring the extract through a strainer or coffee filter. Return the extract and vanilla to the jar.
7. Taste test your extract. Refer to taste testing on page 64.
8. If you desire more coconut, cacao, or almond taste in your extract, add more ingredients by repeating the steps above and storing the jar for an additional 2 months.

Cinnamon Vanilla Extract

Makes about 8 ounces of extract | Extract time: 1 month | Jar size: 8 ounces or larger

Cinnamon, much like vanilla, is a perfect addition to nearly everything sweet and/or baked. Cinnamon rolls, breads, scones, muffins, and so much more. It is also perfect for coffees or hot chocolates to give them a little kick. Or maybe add a splash to your favorite fall or winter cocktail.

Making cinnamon extract is a little different than vanilla extract. Cinnamon sticks can be extracted very quickly, so they don't require the same amount of time as vanilla beans. The simple recipe below will produce a beautiful amber, fragrant, bold cinnamon extract.

2 Ceylon cinnamon sticks

2 Mexican *V. planifolia* vanilla beans

8 ounces white rum

1. Place both cinnamon sticks in the extract jar. Depending on the shape of your jar, you may need to break them in half to ensure that when alcohol is added they will be fully submerged.

2. Slice the vanilla beans lengthwise and add them to the jar. Like the cinnamon, the vanilla beans may need to be cut in half to fit.

3. Pour the rum into the jar, making sure the cinnamon sticks and vanilla beans are completely submerged.

4. Seal the jar and store it in a cool, dark place for 1 month.

After 1 Month

5. Open the extract and simply smell it. If the primary scent is a concentrated, bold cinnamon, your extract is ready. If you feel that it needs more time, reseal the jar and store for another 2 weeks. You can also taste test this extract just as you would with vanilla extract (see page 64).

6. When ready to use, remove the cinnamon sticks. You may need to pour the contents through a strainer if the sticks are breaking apart. While 1 month should be sufficient time, a double-strength extract can be created by adding fresh cinnamon sticks and waiting another 1 month. Leave the vanilla in for added sweetness over time, making sure the beans are cut or folded small enough to remain submerged in the extract.

"Is it wrong to find life's meaning in a cinnamon roll?"
—Keith Wynn

Ginger and Vanilla Spice Extract

Makes about 8 ounces of extract | Extract time: 1 month | Jar size: 12 ounces or larger

This extract not only provides an entirely new, sweet, simple, and brilliant blend of flavors, but it also is a great way to store your unused ginger. In fact, for short-term storage of vanilla beans and ginger, keeping them in alcohol is a great way to preserve them and get the added benefit of flavor within a homemade extract.

This extract is perfect for holiday cooking, beginning with pumpkin bread and cookies in the fall, all the way to gingerbread and even eggnog around Christmastime. You can also add a splash to your stir-fry dishes for enhanced flavor.

1 ounce Tanzanian *V. planifolia* vanilla beans

1 cup peeled, sliced ginger

8 ounces spiced rum

1. Slice the vanilla beans lengthwise, cut them in half, and place them in the jar. Then add the sliced ginger on top.

2. Pour the spiced rum into the jar, making sure the ingredients are completely submerged.

3. Seal the jar and store it in a cool, dark place for 1 month.

After 1 Month

4. Open the extract and smell it. If the primary scent is ginger, your extract is ready. If you feel that it needs more time, reseal the jar and store for another 2 weeks. You can also taste test the extract just as you would with a vanilla extract (see page 64).

5. When ready to use, remove and discard the ginger by pouring the extract through a strainer, then return the extract and the vanilla beans to the jar. Leave the vanilla in for added sweetness over time, making sure the beans are cut or folded small enough to remain submerged in the extract.

"It is the sweet, simple things of life which are the real ones after all."
—Laura Ingalls Wilder

The
KRAKEN
BLACK SPICED
RUM
BIZARRE & FIERCE
Sea Creatures
47% ALC/VOL

Hazelnut and Vanilla Extract

Makes about 8 ounces of extract | Extract time: 3 months | Jar size: 12 ounces or larger

In coffee, bread, cookies, and ice cream, the natural sweetness of hazelnuts is the perfect extract of choice. Especially in homemade chocolate frostings and spreads (think of the hazelnut-based Nutella), there is truly nothing greater than hazelnut extract. This is a simple extract that should be a staple of your at-home cooking arsenal. Our extract-making friend Vickie helped inspire this recipe.

1 cup raw hazelnuts (×2)

2–4 Sri Lankan *V. planifolia* vanilla beans

8 ounces vodka

Note: You can dry the used hazelnuts and blend them into a powder for use in baked goods.

"Baking is done out of love, to share with family and friends, to see them smile."
—Anna Olson

1. Preheat the oven to 220°F.

2. Remove the skins from the hazelnuts by placing them all in a quart-sized mason jar and shaking the jar for a minute or two. Most of the skins will fall off and you can then remove the clean hazelnuts.

3. Place the clean hazelnuts evenly on a baking sheet and bake for 10 minutes. Watch them closely to ensure that they don't burn.

4. Remove the hazelnuts from the oven and place them on a cheesecloth (or a clean dish cloth) to rub the remaining skins from them while they are still warm. Remove as much of the skin as you can, then place the hazelnuts in the extract jar. Any remaining skin pieces will be removed later when you strain the extract.

5. Slice the vanilla beans lengthwise, cut them in half, and add them to the jar.

6. Pour the vodka over the ingredients, ensuring everything is fully submerged.

7. Seal the jar, give it a quick shake, and store it in a cool, dark place for 1 month.

After 1 Month

8. Remove the hazelnuts (see recipe note) by pouring the contents through a strainer. Return the extract and vanilla to the jar.

9. Add fresh hazelnuts by repeating steps 1–4 above, keeping the same vanilla beans in the jar.

10. Reseal the jar and store for 1 month.

After 2 Months

11. Replace the hazelnuts as you did at 1 month, keeping the same vanilla beans.

12. Reseal the jar and store for 1 more month.

After 3 Months

13. Remove the hazelnuts one final time, then return the extract and the vanilla to the jar.

14. Taste test your extract. Refer to taste testing on page 64. If you like the taste, begin using your extract. Keep the vanilla beans in the jar for added sweetness over time, cutting or folding them as necessary so they are fully submerged in the extract at all times.

Pecan Vanilla Extract

Makes about 8 ounces of extract | Extract time: 6 months | Jar size: 12 ounces or larger

Sometimes less is more and simpler is sweeter. This final extract shows how simple extract making really is and how many sweet applications it has. Pecan extract is wonderful in banana bread, pie crusts, masa for tamales, corn bread, pumpkin pies, and, of course, pecan pies.

1 cup whole, shelled pecans (×2)

2 Congo *V. planifolia* vanilla beans (or your favorite)

8 ounces vodka

Note: You can dry the used pecans and blend them into a powder for use in baked goods.

1. Place the pecans in the jar.

2. Slice the vanilla beans lengthwise, cut them in half, and add them to the jar.

3. Pour the vodka over the ingredients, ensuring everything is fully submerged.

4. Seal the jar and store it in a cool, dark place for 3 months.

After 3 Months

5. Pour the contents through a strainer to remove the old pecans (see recipe note). Return the extract and the vanilla beans to the jar.

6. Add 1 cup of new pecans.

7. Reseal the jar and store it in a cool, dark place for 3 more months.

After 6 Months

8. Strain out the pecans and return the extract and vanilla to the jar.

9. Taste test your extract. Refer to taste testing on page 64. It should have a concentrated pecan taste with soft undertones of vanilla. If it is to your liking, then your extract is now ready. If more pecan flavor is desired, then replace the pecans one more time and store for 3 more months, removing the pecans before use. The vanilla can stay in the extract for added sweetness over time; just make sure to cut or fold the beans as necessary so they stay fully submerged at all times.

Used Vanilla Beans

Don't throw away your vanilla beans after your extract is ready! In addition to tossing them in a mother jar, as mentioned on page 54, you can also use them to make vanilla powder, vanilla sugar, or vanilla paste.

Vanilla Bean Powder

Makes about ¼ cup of vanilla bean powder

One of the great lessons of extract making is that we never throw out ingredients after they have been extracted. There is always a use. Especially with expensive vanilla beans. There is always something new that can be made when the extract is finished.

Vanilla bean powder is the perfect example. It's an easy way to get the last bit of sweetness out of used pods. By baking them until they are dry, then pulverizing them in a food processor, we can find even more sweet applications. Vanilla bean powder can be used as a garnish, sprinkled over cakes, frostings, and desserts, and blended into your coffee beans for a sweet morning brew.

1 ounce used, extracted vanilla beans

1. Lay out the used vanilla beans on a baking sheet. Let the beans dry overnight to evaporate the alcohol from the extract.

2. Preheat the oven to 150°F.

3. Bake the vanilla beans for 1 ½ hours. Then remove the sheet from the oven and let the beans cool for 20 minutes.

4. Break the beans into small pieces and place them in a food processor or grinder. Grind them into a fine powder. Your vanilla bean powder is ready for use. Store it unrefrigerated in a sealed container in a cool, dark place. The powder should last for at least 1 year.

Vanilla Bean Sugar

Makes 2 cups of vanilla bean sugar

How do you make sugar even sweeter? By adding vanilla beans, of course. There are so many ways to incorporate vanilla sugar into everyday use. Put it in your coffee, tea, hot cocoa, smoothies, or over fresh fruit. Add it to homemade vanilla ice cream, or sprinkle it over the top of your toast, muffins, or cookies. Bake with it, use it in your sugar scrubs, and so much more!

1 ounce used, extracted vanilla beans

2 cups granulated sugar (or stevia or any type of sugar you choose)

1. If the used vanilla beans are not already sliced open, then slice them open lengthwise and cut them into a few smaller pieces. Leave the vanilla beans on a baking sheet overnight for the alcohol to evaporate.

2. Place the vanilla beans in a food processer with the sugar. Pulse the sugar and vanilla beans until the beans and seeds are well incorporated into the sugar. Your vanilla bean sugar is now ready for use. Store it unrefrigerated in a sealed container in a cool, dark place. Vanilla sugar should last for up to 2 years.

Note: Given the moisture from the used vanilla beans, the sugar may harden and require that you break it up with a spoon before use. You can also use a food processor to break up sugar blocks.

Vanilla Bean Paste

Makes 1 ½ cups of vanilla bean paste

Our last recipe in this book is one of our favorite uses of used vanilla beans. Vanilla bean paste can be much stronger and more flavorful than vanilla extract. It's not difficult to make but does require a little more time to do it right. The vanilla bean paste that you find in grocery stores is often full of unhealthy corn syrup. We want to teach you how to make something cleaner and even sweeter.

Use vanilla bean paste in cream cheese frosting, Bavarian cream, or, our favorite application, homemade vanilla ice cream.

30 used, extracted vanilla beans (4–5 ounces)

6 tablespoons vanilla extract

1 ⅔ cups organic, raw agave nectar (use vegetable glycerin for a sugar-free option)

1. Place the used vanilla beans, vanilla extract, and agave nectar in a food processor and blend until you have a smooth consistency with minimal vanilla "lumps."

2. Place a strainer over a glass jar and pour the blended slurry into the strainer. Using a spoon, press the pulp into the strainer, so a clean, filtered paste falls into the jar.

3. Continue adding and pressing the pulp until it is no longer dripping into the jar. Your vanilla bean paste is now ready for use. Store the paste in an airtight container in a cool, dark place. Do not store it in a refrigerator. Shelf life is usually 1 year.

"My favorite books are the ones that make me smile for hours after reading them. I want that for my readers, for the sweetness to linger."
—Sarah Addison Allen

Veracruz Bourbon
Orange cranberry Everclear
Check in 4 wks
Overproof Rum
Almond Joy
Mocha Vanilla
Vanilla Pecan
Tahiti bourbon
Autumn Spice
Store 30 days

Ugandan Rum
Pineapple Vanilla Vodka
Δ in 2 mos
Indonesian Bourbon
VANILLA PURA
VANILLAPURA
GOURMET VANILLA
and Paul Fulton
Est. 2016
Rum Double fold 8/26
Chocolate Vanilla
√ in 3 mos
Raspberry Van Rum
√ in 4wks
Blackberry Van
Rum √ 3 mos
Tahiti Bourbon
Cherry Chocolate Vanilla Vodka
Remove in 2 mos

Conclusion

When we first began researching vanilla beans and extracts, we never could have imagined the complicated story behind this beautiful little spice. As we uncovered its origins and met thousands of people involved in its cultivation, its distribution, and its many cooking applications, we have been astonished again and again by all that is required for us to simply enjoy the taste of vanilla.

From planting a vine, to pollinating an orchid four years later, to harvesting a bean nine months after that, to conditioning a bean for several months, to finally receiving the vanilla bean in your home, you are experiencing the last step of up to a five-year process. Indeed, the global proliferation of vanilla beans is a modern-day agricultural and logistical marvel that makes this incredible bean the second-most-expensive spice in the world.

Most importantly and enjoyably, our journey has allowed us to associate with people around the world that make a living from this miraculous little bean. Every morning in the world's bean belt, thousands of people wake up and go to work on the farms that produce these beautiful vanilla beans. If harsh weather destroys their fields, if economic uncertainty slows demand, and if political unrest disrupts vanilla bean distribution, then these farmers and laborers can't earn sufficient income to sustain their families.

And so it is that in our global economy, when someone in the world purchases one ounce of vanilla beans from any source, those dollars make it back to villages in Madagascar, Uganda, Vanuatu, Tahiti, Tonga, the Cook Islands, Sri Lanka, Tanzania, Ecuador, Mexico, the Congo, and dozens of other regions around our ever-shrinking planet. And because of that purchase, a family in one of these countries has food on their table and an opportunity for a better life.

In February of 2022, we received this handwritten letter from one of our vanilla bean farmers:

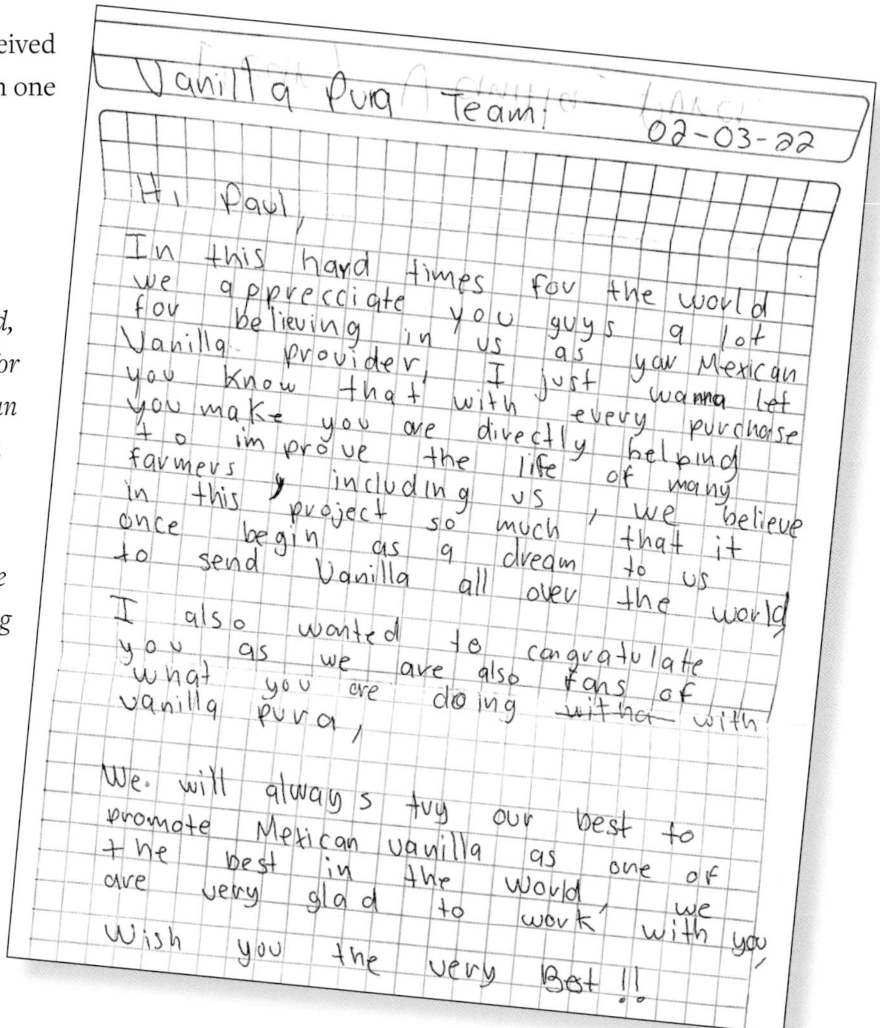
Vanilla Pura Team: 02-03-22

Hi Paul,

In this hard times for the world we appreciate you guys a lot for believing in us as your Mexican Vanilla provider, I just wanna let you know that with every purchase you make you are directly helping to improve the life of many farmers, including us in this project so much, we believe once begin as a dream to us to send Vanilla all over the world

I also wanted to congratulate you as we are also fans of what you are doing ~~with the~~ with vanilla pura,

We will always try our best to promote Mexican vanilla as one of the best in the world, we are very glad to work with you,

Wish you the very Best!!

VanillaPura Team:

Hi Paul,

In this hard time for the world, we appreciate you guys a lot for believing in us as your Mexican vanilla provider. I just wanna let you know that with every purchase you make you are directly helping to improve the life of many farmers, including us. We believe in this project so much that it once began as a dream to us to send vanilla all over the world.

I also wanted to congratulate you, as we are also fans of what you are doing with VanillaPura.

We will always try our best to promote Mexican vanilla as one of the best in the world. We are very glad to work with you.

Everything we do has an impact on someone else. We are so thankful to be part of something that provides happiness from the farm to the kitchen for people all around the world. Indeed, we are all making the world sweeter, one vanilla bean at a time.

Acknowledgments

Grandma Due

In her 88th year, Jill's mother, "Grandma Due," applied our logo labels to thousands of shipping envelopes for our many vanilla bean orders. She wouldn't let us outsource that job as our business grew because it was an opportunity for her to visit our home and spend time with Jill and her grandsons. And seldom did she arrive without chocolate muffins for the boys and stories about Papa Due. Thank you, Grandma Due, for being such a sweet part of our story.

Teresa

Jill's sister Teresa lives more than an hour from our home. In countless moments when Jill was overwhelmed with a project related to this book and our business, Teresa would drop everything and spend a day, an afternoon, and/or an evening helping Jill because, as she would often say, "That's just what sisters do." She continues to be an integral part of our business today. Thank you, Teresa, for being you.

Our Family

Thanks to all our family that have encouraged us as we pursued our sweet little hobby that has filled so much of our life. Many of your ideas are found in practice within this book and within our business. Thank you for cheering us on when we shipped our first order, and for being the very first recipients of our vanilla beans and extracts.

Judi and Wendy

Amid a difficult day, or week or month, Jill always has a light at the end of the tunnel. That light is "hair night," when Jill can spend several hours with Judi and their talented hair stylist and friend, Wendy, who has been styling their hair for more than twenty years. It was during "hair night" in 2016 that the idea of making vanilla extract for Christmas gifts was first discussed. We have been trying to help others duplicate that magical, extract-making experience ever since.

Jenny Woods

Paul has worked with Jenny since 1999. She is our talented graphic designer that, through two decades, has patiently listened to our crazy ideas and has managed to bring them to life through her beautiful, artistic, creative mind. She has transformed our words into colors and a brand. Her beautiful art reflects the ideals that we have always pursued of kindness, quality, and beauty within simplicity.

Starlette and Our Virtual Vanilla Family

We met Starlette Balsoma Connelly virtually in October of 2020 when we started our extract-making group on Facebook called "Making Vanilla Extract by VanillaPura." She immediately became part of our vanilla family, as one of the most creative and innovative extract makers in our group. She was the inspiration behind several extract recipes that incorporate entirely new uses of vanilla, spices, and more. Thank you, Starlette, for your never-ending sweetness and bold creativity. You really are a star.

Several other members of our online group have contributed recipes, feedback, inspiration, and insights for years now. Laura Achten, Shannon Adams, Therese Di Carlo Bach, Ruth Batten, Callie Beeson, Duane Brisendine, Nadira Brown, Ann Bushon, Allen Clabo, Vicki DeGaetano, Cathy Donaldson, Bonnie Foskey, Krista Howard, Jeanette Ionge, Dawn Knauss, Roxanna Kuusala, Mark Lally, Lori Lanford, Ruth Lord, John J. Meyer, Michelle Pojeta, Keri Seibert, Jeff Sewell, Carol Stormer, Mary Elizabeth Terberg, Debbie Perry Thomas, Ramona Wysong, Roxann Young, and so many others who inspired many of these recipes and were early participants in our online community. We thank you all for sharing your creativity and your sweetness with us. As Starlette always says, "Vanilla is our YUM!!"

Nick Sokoloff

Our talented photographer that captured our craft through complicated uses of light and ingredients and glass, and brilliantly captured the purity of the art of making extracts at home.

Dana and Bill Bunn, Emily and John Harrison

Thank you for always reminding us to live out loud, to laugh, to enjoy today, and to strive confidently and unceasingly to build a better world, starting with the world around us.

My Extract Journal

These pages are for you to keep track of your extract creations over time.

Extract name:			
Name of recipe followed:			
Start date:	Day: Month: Year:		
Vanilla bean origin:			
Vanilla bean species:			
Vanilla bean grade (A or B):	A or B	Single, double, or triple fold:	
Vanilla bean prep (circle one):	Cut Left whole Split Knotted Other:		
Order date:	Day: Month: Year:		
Ordered from:			
Price of beans/oz:		Number of beans/oz:	
Alcohol used:		Cost of alcohol used:	
List other ingredients used & cost:			
Total cost per batch:			
Shake monthly (if desired):	JAN FEB MAR APR MAY JUN JUL AUG SEP OCT NOV DEC		
Expected completion date:	Day: Month: Year:		
Dates and results of taste tests:	1. 2. 3.		
Approved for use date:	Day: Month: Year:		
Miscellaneous notes:			

Extract name:			
Name of recipe followed:			
Start date:	Day: Month: Year:		
Vanilla bean origin:			
Vanilla bean species:			
Vanilla bean grade (A or B):	A or B	Single, double, or triple fold:	
Vanilla bean prep (circle one):	Cut Left whole Split Knotted Other:		
Order date:	Day: Month: Year:		
Ordered from:			
Price of beans/oz:		Number of beans/oz:	
Alcohol used:		Cost of alcohol used:	
List other ingredients used & cost:			
Total cost per batch:			
Shake monthly (if desired):	JAN FEB MAR APR MAY JUN JUL AUG SEP OCT NOV DEC		
Expected completion date:	Day: Month: Year:		
Dates and results of taste tests:	1. 2. 3.		
Approved for use date:	Day: Month: Year:		
Miscellaneous notes:			

Extract name:			
Name of recipe followed:			
Start date:	Day: Month: Year:		
Vanilla bean origin:			
Vanilla bean species:			
Vanilla bean grade (A or B):	A or B	Single, double, or triple fold:	
Vanilla bean prep (circle one):	Cut Left whole Split Knotted Other:		
Order date:	Day: Month: Year:		
Ordered from:			
Price of beans/oz:		Number of beans/oz:	
Alcohol used:		Cost of alcohol used:	
List other ingredients used & cost:			
Total cost per batch:			
Shake monthly (if desired):	JAN FEB MAR APR MAY JUN JUL AUG SEP OCT NOV DEC		
Expected completion date:	Day: Month: Year:		
Dates and results of taste tests:	1. 2. 3.		
Approved for use date:	Day: Month: Year:		
Miscellaneous notes:			

Extract name:	
Name of recipe followed:	
Start date:	Day: Month: Year:
Vanilla bean origin:	
Vanilla bean species:	
Vanilla bean grade (A or B):	A or B — Single, double, or triple fold:
Vanilla bean prep (circle one):	Cut Left whole Split Knotted Other:
Order date:	Day: Month: Year:
Ordered from:	
Price of beans/oz:	Number of beans/oz:
Alcohol used:	Cost of alcohol used:
List other ingredients used & cost:	
Total cost per batch:	
Shake monthly (if desired):	JAN FEB MAR APR MAY JUN JUL AUG SEP OCT NOV DEC
Expected completion date:	Day: Month: Year:
Dates and results of taste tests:	1. 2. 3.
Approved for use date:	Day: Month: Year:
Miscellaneous notes:	

Extract name:			
Name of recipe followed:			
Start date:	Day: Month: Year:		
Vanilla bean origin:			
Vanilla bean species:			
Vanilla bean grade (A or B):	A or B	Single, double, or triple fold:	
Vanilla bean prep (circle one):	Cut Left whole Split Knotted Other:		
Order date:	Day: Month: Year:		
Ordered from:			
Price of beans/oz:		Number of beans/oz:	
Alcohol used:		Cost of alcohol used:	
List other ingredients used & cost:			
Total cost per batch:			
Shake monthly (if desired):	JAN FEB MAR APR MAY JUN JUL AUG SEP OCT NOV DEC		
Expected completion date:	Day: Month: Year:		
Dates and results of taste tests:	1. 2. 3.		
Approved for use date:	Day: Month: Year:		
Miscellaneous notes:			

Extract name:			
Name of recipe followed:			
Start date:	Day: Month: Year:		
Vanilla bean origin:			
Vanilla bean species:			
Vanilla bean grade (A or B):	A or B	Single, double, or triple fold:	
Vanilla bean prep (circle one):	Cut Left whole Split Knotted Other:		
Order date:	Day: Month: Year:		
Ordered from:			
Price of beans/oz:		Number of beans/oz:	
Alcohol used:		Cost of alcohol used:	
List other ingredients used & cost:			
Total cost per batch:			
Shake monthly (if desired):	JAN FEB MAR APR MAY JUN JUL AUG SEP OCT NOV DEC		
Expected completion date:	Day: Month: Year:		
Dates and results of taste tests:	1. 2. 3.		
Approved for use date:	Day: Month: Year:		
Miscellaneous notes:			

Extract name:			
Name of recipe followed:			
Start date:	Day: Month: Year:		
Vanilla bean origin:			
Vanilla bean species:			
Vanilla bean grade (A or B):	A or B	Single, double, or triple fold:	
Vanilla bean prep (circle one):	Cut Left whole Split Knotted Other:		
Order date:	Day: Month: Year:		
Ordered from:			
Price of beans/oz:		Number of beans/oz:	
Alcohol used:		Cost of alcohol used:	
List other ingredients used & cost:			
Total cost per batch:			
Shake monthly (if desired):	JAN FEB MAR APR MAY JUN JUL AUG SEP OCT NOV DEC		
Expected completion date:	Day: Month: Year:		
Dates and results of taste tests:	1. 2. 3.		
Approved for use date:	Day: Month: Year:		
Miscellaneous notes:			

Extract name:			
Name of recipe followed:			
Start date:	Day: Month: Year:		
Vanilla bean origin:			
Vanilla bean species:			
Vanilla bean grade (A or B):	A or B	Single, double, or triple fold:	
Vanilla bean prep (circle one):	Cut Left whole Split Knotted Other:		
Order date:	Day: Month: Year:		
Ordered from:			
Price of beans/oz:		Number of beans/oz:	
Alcohol used:		Cost of alcohol used:	
List other ingredients used & cost:			
Total cost per batch:			
Shake monthly (if desired):	JAN FEB MAR APR MAY JUN JUL AUG SEP OCT NOV DEC		
Expected completion date:	Day: Month: Year:		
Dates and results of taste tests:	1. 2. 3.		
Approved for use date:	Day: Month: Year:		
Miscellaneous notes:			

Extract name:			
Name of recipe followed:			
Start date:	Day: Month: Year:		
Vanilla bean origin:			
Vanilla bean species:			
Vanilla bean grade (A or B):	A or B	Single, double, or triple fold:	
Vanilla bean prep (circle one):	Cut Left whole Split Knotted Other:		
Order date:	Day: Month: Year:		
Ordered from:			
Price of beans/oz:		Number of beans/oz:	
Alcohol used:		Cost of alcohol used:	
List other ingredients used & cost:			
Total cost per batch:			
Shake monthly (if desired):	JAN FEB MAR APR MAY JUN JUL AUG SEP OCT NOV DEC		
Expected completion date:	Day: Month: Year:		
Dates and results of taste tests:	1. 2. 3.		
Approved for use date:	Day: Month: Year:		
Miscellaneous notes:			

Extract name:			
Name of recipe followed:			
Start date:	Day: Month: Year:		
Vanilla bean origin:			
Vanilla bean species:			
Vanilla bean grade (A or B):	A or B	Single, double, or triple fold:	
Vanilla bean prep (circle one):	Cut Left whole Split Knotted Other:		
Order date:	Day: Month: Year:		
Ordered from:			
Price of beans/oz:		Number of beans/oz:	
Alcohol used:		Cost of alcohol used:	
List other ingredients used & cost:			
Total cost per batch:			
Shake monthly (if desired):	JAN FEB MAR APR MAY JUN JUL AUG SEP OCT NOV DEC		
Expected completion date:	Day: Month: Year:		
Dates and results of taste tests:	1. 2. 3.		
Approved for use date:	Day: Month: Year:		
Miscellaneous notes:			

Extract name:			
Name of recipe followed:			
Start date:	Day: Month: Year:		
Vanilla bean origin:			
Vanilla bean species:			
Vanilla bean grade (A or B):	A or B	Single, double, or triple fold:	
Vanilla bean prep (circle one):	Cut Left whole Split Knotted Other:		
Order date:	Day: Month: Year:		
Ordered from:			
Price of beans/oz:		Number of beans/oz:	
Alcohol used:		Cost of alcohol used:	
List other ingredients used & cost:			
Total cost per batch:			
Shake monthly (if desired):	JAN FEB MAR APR MAY JUN JUL AUG SEP OCT NOV DEC		
Expected completion date:	Day: Month: Year:		
Dates and results of taste tests:	1. 2. 3.		
Approved for use date:	Day: Month: Year:		
Miscellaneous notes:			

Extract name:			
Name of recipe followed:			
Start date:	Day: Month: Year:		
Vanilla bean origin:			
Vanilla bean species:			
Vanilla bean grade (A or B):	A or B	Single, double, or triple fold:	
Vanilla bean prep (circle one):	Cut Left whole Split Knotted Other:		
Order date:	Day: Month: Year:		
Ordered from:			
Price of beans/oz:		Number of beans/oz:	
Alcohol used:		Cost of alcohol used:	
List other ingredients used & cost:			
Total cost per batch:			
Shake monthly (if desired):	JAN FEB MAR APR MAY JUN JUL AUG SEP OCT NOV DEC		
Expected completion date:	Day: Month: Year:		
Dates and results of taste tests:	1. 2. 3.		
Approved for use date:	Day: Month: Year:		
Miscellaneous notes:			

Extract name:	
Name of recipe followed:	
Start date:	Day: Month: Year:
Vanilla bean origin:	
Vanilla bean species:	
Vanilla bean grade (A or B):	A or B **Single, double, or triple fold:**
Vanilla bean prep (circle one):	Cut Left whole Split Knotted Other:
Order date:	Day: Month: Year:
Ordered from:	
Price of beans/oz:	**Number of beans/oz:**
Alcohol used:	**Cost of alcohol used:**
List other ingredients used & cost:	
Total cost per batch:	
Shake monthly (if desired):	JAN FEB MAR APR MAY JUN JUL AUG SEP OCT NOV DEC
Expected completion date:	Day: Month: Year:
Dates and results of taste tests:	1. 2. 3.
Approved for use date:	Day: Month: Year:
Miscellaneous notes:	

Index

D

E

F

G

H

I

J

K

L

M

N

O

P

R

S

T

About the Authors

Paul and Jill Fulton started VanillaPura in 2016. Their passion for extract making helped them develop a business, a large online community, and a center for helpful extract-making content.

VanillaPura became a place where kindness and sweetness to others always comes first. Their social media following grew by more than 100,000 people in one year. Each person within their online community has committed to be kind and sweet to all others. VanillaPura's Facebook group is often referred to as "the happiest place on Facebook."

Jill is a Registered Nurse by education. After graduating with a Bachelor of Science in Nursing degree in 1998, she worked in the Adult Intensive Care Units of several hospitals for seven years. Her passion was patient care—making sure that she always gave every ounce of her energy to those under her watch. She stepped away from her career in 2004 to focus exclusively on raising her two sons. Her career in business is an unexpected one, as much of VanillaPura's growth fell on her shoulders. She quickly learned to manage operations, production, fulfillment, and customer service.

Paul has been in business his entire life. He spent the first fifteen years of his career in the Caribbean and global resort markets, opening retail stores in more than one hundred locations and twenty-two countries around the world. He has worked as the president and CEO of various businesses within resort retail, manufacturing, and ecommerce. Paul graduated from the University of Utah with a degree in marketing in 2002, and then an Executive MBA in 2007.

When Paul and Jill aren't making and using their extracts, or working on their business, you will find them in the mountains near their home hiking, mountain biking, skiing, and fly fishing. They reside in Highland, Utah, with their two sons, Tommy and Sam, as well as Maggie, their Golden Retriever.